COST – the acronym for European COoperation in Science and Technology – is the oldest and widest European intergovernmental network for cooperation in research. Established by the Ministerial Conference in November 1971, COST is presently used by the scientific communities of 36 European countries to cooperate in common research projects supported by national funds.

The funds provided by COST – less than 1% of the total value of the projects – support the COST cooperation networks (COST Actions) through which, with EUR 30 million per year, more than 30.000 European scientists are involved in research having a total value which exceeds EUR 2 billion per year. This is the financial worth of the European added value which COST achieves.

A "bottom up approach" (the initiative of launching a COST Action comes from the European scientists themselves), "à la carte participation" (only countries interested in the Action participate), "equality of access" (participation is open also to the scientific communities of countries not belonging to the European Union) and "flexible structure" (easy implementation and light management of the research initiatives) are the main characteristics of COST.

As precursor of advanced multidisciplinary research COST has a very important role for the realisation of the European Research Area (ERA) anticipating and complementing the activities of the Framework Programmes, constituting a "bridge" towards the scientific communities of emerging countries, increasing the mobility of researchers across Europe and fostering the establishment of "Networks of Excellence" in many key scientific domains such as: Biomedicine and Molecular Biosciences; Food and Agriculture; Forests, their Products and Services; Materials, Physical and Nanosciences; Chemistry and Molecular Sciences and Technologies; Earth System Science and Environmental Management; Information and Communication Technologies; Transport and Urban Development; Individuals, Societies, Cultures and Health. It covers basic and more applied research and also addresses issues of pre-normative nature or of societal importance.

Web: http://www.cost.eu

ESF Provides the COST Office through an EC contract

COST is supported by the EU RTD Framework programme

Davide Rocchesso
Università IUAV di Venezia
Dorsoduro 2206
30123 Venezia, Italia

©COST Office and Logos Verlag Berlin GmbH, 2011
COST Reference Number: PUB 1159
No permission to reproduce or utilise the contents of this book by any means is
necessary, other than in the case of images, diagrammes or other material from
other copyright holders. In such cases, permission of the copyright holders is
required. This book may be cited as:

Davide Rocchesso. *Explorations in Sonic Interaction Design*. COST Office. Logos
Verlag, Berlin, Germany, 2011.

The   Sonic Interaction Design **SI)**   logo has been designed by Frauke Behrendt.

The Deutsche Nationalbibliothek lists this publication in the Deutsche
Nationalbibliografie; detailed bibliographic data are available in the Internet at
http://dnb.d-nb.de.

ISBN 978-3-8325-2858-4

Logos Verlag Berlin GmbH
Comeniushof, Gubener Str. 47,
10243 Berlin
Tel.: +49 (0)30 42 85 10 90
Fax: +49 (0)30 42 85 10 92
INTERNET: http://www.logos-verlag.de

Davide Rocchesso

Explorations in
Sonic Interaction Design

λογος

Davide Rocchesso
Università IUAV di Venezia
Dorsoduro 2206
30123 Venezia, Italia

Davide Rocchesso. *Explorations in Sonic Interaction Design.* COST Office. Logos
Verlag, Berlin, Germany, 2011.

The 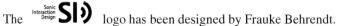 logo has been designed by Frauke Behrendt.

The Deutsche Nationalbibliothek lists this publication in the Deutsche
Nationalbibliografie; detailed bibliographic data are available in the Internet at
http://dnb.d-nb.de.

ISBN 978-3-8325-2858-4

Logos Verlag Berlin GmbH
Comeniushof, Gubener Str. 47,
10243 Berlin
Tel.: +49 (0)30 42 85 10 90
Fax: +49 (0)30 42 85 10 92
INTERNET: http://www.logos-verlag.de

Preface

I have to admit that the initial proposal five years ago was outrageous: making designers focus their attention and efforts onto the sound of interactions - especially those designers who had been striving against unwanted noises, who dreamed of clean and silent mechanisms but involuntarily filled the world with beeps and bleeps.

Five years later, many of these designers have become aware of the informational, expressive, and aesthetic potential of sound in interaction. And the widespread concern about sound pollution is gaining strength and precision by the realization that the quality of soundscapes is much more than a matter of decibels. Thoughtfully designed sounding objects can make our lives and environments better.

The COST Action IC0601 on Sonic Interaction Design (SID: 2007-2011) has made a major contribution to this change of attitude toward sound in interaction, and opened many research threads in design, art, behavioral sciences, and engineering. Over the four years of its activities, many researchers have been engaged in experimental workshops, hands-on training schools, and scientific missions. This book summarizes most of these activities in an attempt to outline the most relevant trends emerging, bottom-up, from the SID community.

Writing this book meant digesting an impressive amount of high-quality material, provided by SID participants. If I have overlooked some of the research results or failed to describe them properly, these omissions, as well as mistakes or imperfections, should be attributed to me, although my aim was to credit all contributors and to refer to their published articles. All of the pictures in this book are taken from the reports, slides or blogs that the participants prepared during SID activities. Being part of an emerging community such as SID means agreeing in sharing and disseminating everybody's work.

The COST Office energetically supported the Action throughout the four years all the way to the final event and exhibition at the Norwegian Museum of Science and Technology. The Science Officers – Afonso Ferreira, Julia Stamm, Gian Mario Maggio, Francesca Boscolo, Jamsheed Shorish, and Matteo Razzanelli – tirelessly encouraged our research activities even when they challenged the boundaries of the Information and Communication Domain. And for making everything run smoothly even in the most hectic times we particularly thank Maria Grazia Ballerano, much more than a Grant Holder's secretary.

Sonic Interaction Design[1] was a new locution five years ago. Nowadays it is a community, a discipline, a brand, and even an attitude of mind. You did a great job SIDers!

This publication is supported by COST.

Venezia, *Davide Rocchesso*
May, 2011

---

[1] http://en.wikipedia.org/wiki/Sonic_interaction_design

Contributors

The chapters of this book have been written starting from the many articles and reports produced during the four years of the COST IC-0601 Action on Sonic Interaction Design. The authors of such materials are listed here, together with the chapters where their work has been described.

Chapter 1   Davide Rocchesso, Stefania Serafin, Frauke Behrendt, Nicola Bernardini, Roberto Bresin, Gerhard Eckel, Karmen Franinovic, Thomas Hermann, Sandra Pauletto, Patrick Susini, and Yon Visell;

Chapter 2   Karmen Franinovic, Lalya Gaye, and Frauke Behrendt;

Chapter 3   Sandra Pauletto, Daniel Hug, Stephen Barrass, and Mary Luckhurst;

Chapter 4   Inger Ekman and Michal Rinott;

Chapter 5   Roberto Bresin, Andy Hunt, and Thomas Hermann;

Chapter 6   Thomas Hermann;

Chapter 7   Fabien Gouyon;

Chapter 8   Cumhur Erkut, Stefano Delle Monache, Daniel Hug, and Davide Rocchesso;

Chapter 9   Heidi-Maria Lehtonen, Stefano Zambon, Balázs Bank, Federico Fontana, Stefano Papetti, Mathieu Lagrange, Matthias Rath, James McDermott, Julien Castet, and Tommaso Bianco;

Chapter 10   Luis Gustavo Martins, Ming Yang, Cécile Picard, Thomas Hermann, and Eoin Brazil;

Chapter 11   Renzo Vitale, Pietro Polotti, and João Cordeiro;

Chapter 12   Martin Rumori, Johanna Gampe, Daniël Ploeger, and Jan Schacher;

Chapter 13   Sandra Pauletto, Michal Rinott, Mariana Julieta López, Loïc Kessous, Karmen Franinovic, Tal Drori, Enrico Costanza, Stefano Delle Monache, and Daniel Hug;

Chapter 14   Kristian Nymoen, Alexander Refsum Jensenius, Tim Redfern, Richard Widerberg, and Rolf Nordahl;

Chapter 15   Florian Grond, Stephan Baumann, Nina Schaffert, Stephen Barrass, and Louise Valgerður Nickerson;

Chapter 16   Suguru Goto, João Lobato Oliveira, Stefania Serafin, Birgit Gasteiger, Luca Turchet, and Bart Moens;

Chapter 17   Kjetil Falkenberg Hansen, Smilen Dimitrov, Jean-Julien Filatriau, and Dan Overholt;

Chapter 18   Norbert Schnell, Esteban Maestre, Stella Paschalidou, Otso Lähdeoja, Baptiste Caramiaux, Luiz Naveda, and Yago De Quay;

Chapter 19   Frauke Behrendt and Trond Lossius.

Contents

Acronyms

COST	COoperation in Science and Technology
ESR	Early-Stage Researcher
MC	Management Committee
NIME	New Interfaces for Musical Expression
SID	Sonic Interaction Design
SMC	Sound and Music Computing
STSM	Short-Term Scientific Mission
TS	Training School
WG	Working Group

Part I
Workshops

Chapter 1
Sound, information, and experience

Abstract Sonic Interaction Design is about practice and inquiry into the roles that sound may play between users and artifacts, services, or environments, in applications that range from the critical functionality of an alarm, to the artistic significance of a musical creation. A workshop at the CHI 2008 Conference in Florence helped defining the perimeter of this discipline.

1.1 Setting the perimeter of Sonic Interaction Design

Sounds continuously mediate many human-object interactions. For example, to describe his favorite juicer Bill Buxton couples sound, proprioception, and action when saying that "There is a cadence in the action that is almost musical" [13].

Sonic Interaction Design explores ways in which sound can be used to convey information, meaning, aesthetic and emotional qualities in interactive contexts. It is a discipline that emerges from contributions coming from different directions, such as auditory display and sonification [63], sound and music computing [108, 135], perception and action [72]. The emergence of the discipline of Sonic Interaction Design is facilitated by the possibilities offered by sensor and actuator technologies. Complex body gestures can nowadays be captured, processed, and tightly coupled to interactive sounds.

The COST Action IC0601 on Sonic Interaction Design promoted a workshop at the CHI conference in Florence in 2008, aimed at defining the perimeter of the discipline through a call for contributions [116]. The selected presentations are described in section 1.2. A further call for papers for a special issue of the International Journal on Human-Computer Studies was launched after the workshop, and six out of twenty submissions were selected for publication [115]. These are described in section 1.3.

1.2 Contributions

The CHI Workshop on Sonic Interaction Design held in Florence in 2008 had a key importance for the development of several research paths in Sonic Interaction Design. This is clear from a quick analysis of the presentations and how they evolved in the following years.

Rocchesso and Polotti [113] drew the attention on continuous interaction and multisensory feedback as key ingredients for successful artifacts of the future. They argued that the method of basic design can be used to tackle the complexity of sonic interactive objects. This approach was further developed through various example cases [114].

Hug [55], from a designer standpoint, described the research fields that are considered relevant for making sense of the design process of sounds for interactive commodities. An initial classification of such commodities was given and exploited in later studies by the same author [56].

A pedagogical viewpoint was taken by Nordahl et al. [91]. They argued that the challenge in interaction design (and especially with sound as a focus) is not *how* to design but *what* and *why* to design. This justifies their approach to teaching, called Problem Based Learning [61], which collects disciplines, notions, and skills around contextualized design problems.

The work of Bresin et al. [12] is part of a long series of efforts to develop sound models that are suitable for continuous auditory feedback in human-object interaction and manipulation. In particular, they proposed a control model for synthesizing crumpling sounds, that proved to be generalizable to many enactive and ecological interfaces, such as foot-floor interaction. This and other sound modeling studies where eventually included in the Sound Design Toolkit [24], now widely used in the Sonic Interaction Design community.

That sound can be an indispensable ingredient for enhancing the sense of presence and immersion in virtual environments was shown by Nordahl [87]. Especially when the visual display is very realistic, as in image-based rendering, the limited mobility of the user needs to be compensated with audio-haptic displays. Experiments show that the subjects move more when dynamic sound sources and sound of ergomotion are rendered in the environment.

Sonification deals with methods, tools, and techniques to convey information to humans by means of sound. Sound models may be used for this purpose (model-based sonification) and data exploration may occur through continuous manipulation of their parameters (interactive sonification). Hermann et al. [54] presented an attemp to organize existing cases of interactive sonification through a software tool that may assist in the generation of new scenarios and designs. Over the last few years, the body of experiences and knowledge in sonification has been collected in the Sonification Handbook [53].

Sound design plays an important role in all performing arts, where historical context and cultural traditions can not be ignored. Chris Salter, the author of Entangled: Technology and Transformation of Performance [119], presented some recent experiences of adaptive audio scenography, where sound is the complex result of environmental sensing, dynamical system evolution, audience-performer co-action, and designed dramaturgical structure [118].

The perception-action loop becomes particularly complex and challenging when sensors capture physiological signals, and such signals are mapped to auditory displays. Erkut et al. [31] showed how such entanglement could be, at least partially, resolved through several days of hands-on workshop.

By the end of the twentieth century, the availability of accessible microcontrollers, sensors, and tools contributed to creating a new wave of do-it-yourself enthusiasts. As part of this movement, a community of researchers and practitioners in New Interfaces for Musical Expression[1] was created and has been holding its annual conference since 2001. How relevant this is for Sonic Interaction Design was explained by Crevoisier [21], who presented the Future Instruments network[2].

Science can come very close to art when an interdisciplinary group of people work together to provide an immersive audio-visual experience of massive multi-dimensional scientific data. This is what Wakefield et al. have been doing with the AlloBrain, an environment designed for a specific facility (the AlloSphere) at the University of California, Santa Barbara. The contribution presented at the workshop in Florence [144] evolved into a journal publication [136].

The sounds of interaction are very often non-musical, and related to our everyday experience. As far as the scientific understanding of auditory perception and psychoacoustics is concerned, much is known about musical sounds that would be interesting to transfer to the realm of everyday sounds. This is what Minard et al. [82] did about the perception of timbres, by extending the methods of investigation originally developed for musical timbres.

Important examples of how research in Sonic Interaction Desing and auditory display translates (and more often does not translate) into actual products was given by Ronkainen of Nokia [117]. His contribution was concluded by a set of questions for the research community that are here replicated:

- How to design small, unobtrusive sounds that convey their meaning for the user but avoid catching the attention of others unnecessarily?
- How to present different levels of urgency with sounds while allowing enough freedom for sound design?
- How to find best ways of matching sound design with overall product design?

---

[1] http://www.nime.org
[2] http://future-instruments.net

5

- How to apply the research on auditory user interface design on commercial product design so that the requirements above are met?

These are still open issues for the Sonic Interaction Design community.

1.3 A journal special issue

The International Journal of Human-Computer Studies published in 2009 a special issue [115] that gives a faithful, albeit incomplete, picture of some issues that are central to contemporary research in Sonic Interaction Design. The six selected articles range from issues in sonification and auditory display, to applications in artistic and product design contexts, to evaluation techniques for sonic interaction design.

Frauenberger and Stockman [41] start from the literature of auditory display to look for compelling design patterns that could be used in Sonic Interaction Design. They propose context as a design principle that allows transfer of good practices from experts to novices.

Pauletto and Hunt [101] take an information sonification direction and give two examples of sonification of complex medical data, where interaction is functional to data exploration both for offline analysis and for real-time monitoring.

The topic of interactive exploration of complex datasets through sound – called interactive sonification – is also treated by Thompson et al. [136]. In particular, they document the design and development of a large immersive environment, called the Allobrain, where sound is a key ingredient for the exploration of complex structures arising from fMRI brain data.

Visell et al. [142] look at interactions that occur at the interface between feet and floor, and survey the literature of display and perception of walking generated sounds and vibrations. They also point to potential future applications, where sonic augmentation of shoes or tiles could produce new experiences of walking. This is an area where interaction design works at the interface between, humans, objects, and environments.

Stowell et al. [134] present a work that expresses the need of practitioners in music and multimedia performing arts to have means to evaluate sonic interactive systems. Qualitative methods – such as discourse analysis – as well as quantitative methods are proposed and contrasted to other evaluation approaches.

From a stance rooted in experimental psychology, Lemaitre et al. [71] propose a new approach to the evaluation of the designed sonic feedback in objects that are subject to continuous manipulation. The originality of their contribution is in the use of an abstract object that allows controlled experimentation of an interaction primitive.

Chapter 2
Sonic Interaction Design in everyday contexts

Abstract The first of a series of design workshops promoted by the COST Action on Sonic Interaction Design was held as part of the International Conference on Auditory Display in 2008. The rationale of design workshops is that participants get an embodied understanding of the challenges of designing for meaningful and engaging physical interaction with computational sonic artifacts. This kind of embodied knowledge is thought to complement cognition and technology-based approaches.

2.1 Research through workshops

The first of a series of hands-on workshops promoted by the COST Action on Sonic Interaction Design was held in Paris on June 23rd, 2008, as part of the International Conference on Auditory Display. It tackled one of the key problems in Sonic Interaction Design, that is design for continuous feedback in tangible artifacts. The workshop was designed to explore everyday sounding objects in context. Concepts and scenarios for future products were collaboratively conceived, through design exercises. Participants explored the meanings and importance of tangible sonic interactions in a variety of contexts and imagined how such contexts might be changed through designed sounds. Techniques such as bodystorming and interaction relabeling were used [95, 27].

A one-day workshop can be structured in four parts: warm-up exercises, creative idea generation, concept exploration, and final presentation and discussion. While the whole workshop can be run without any digital technology, it can be expanded into several days of activities, including extensive prototyping with sensors, actuators, and computing elements.

2.2 Warm-up exercises

Each participant was asked to bring a sound-making object and to reproduce its sound without using the object itself. This is an embryo of sonic sketching (see section 4), using readily-available resources such as the voice, the body, or other objects. Then, participants were asked to sketch, with paper and pencil, sounds of the urban environment as well as silent objects that are potential candidates for being augmented with sound. Finally, a play table for audio-haptic exploration of objects was arranged and participants, divided in couples, shared their experiences.

Fig. 2.1 Sounding objects for warm-up exercise

2.3 Idea generation

In the early stage of the design process, brainstorming sessions are a common mean to generate a large number of ideas. In this workshop, a particularly productive kind of brainstorming, called speed dating, was used. It was based on a multidimensional matrix of design parameters, in this case being a location (kitchen, street, etc.), an activity (walking, drinking, etc.) and an artifact (umbrella, glass, chair, etc.). The latter were physical objects which enabled participants to quickly bodystorm their ideas. Working in pairs that change every ten minutes, the participants quickly filled the matrix of design ideas (see figure 2.2). In this way the participants interacted with each other through conceptualization phase under a time constraint.

Fig. 2.2 Filling a design matrix through speed dating

2.4 Concept exploration and presentation

In the third phase of the workshop, some selected concepts from design matrix were explored in small group sessions. Interaction relabeling was used to map possible interactions with an object to sonic behaviors of computational artifacts to be designed, and cultural issues were taken into consideration by having the participants perform as extreme characters. The Non-Verbal Scenarios method allowed participants to quickly communicate and discuss their design concepts. In it, participants were allowed to present their interactive concepts by acting out an experience without the use of words, but only by making simulating sonic feedback. Performative acts for Sonic Interaction Design have been addressed by a specific workshop in 2009 (see chapter 3).

2.5 Results

A final workshop discussion allowed circulation of ideas and impressions, as well as formation of a consensus on the most relevant results. In addition to immediate discussion, written questionnaires were submitted via email, several months after the workshop. Participants reported that playful strategies stimulated their imagination; helped them relax; allowed them to forget about disciplinary differences;

and facilitated networking with other participants. Warm-up and field methods were seen as a very valuable way to start thinking about the experience with sonic objects. One of the most difficult tasks was to talk about the sonic aspects of an interactive object. The alternatives to written or spoken word proved to enrich and complement the existing sound classifications and terminology. For example, in the Sonic Postcards exercise, when visually expressing a sonic experience in urban contexts, participants with different backgrounds chose different representations. The variety of media and expressive options ensured that the required skills do not privilege a certain discipline. The presence of objects and the use of voice were highly appreciated by the participants and proved to be the most valuable solutions to this problem. The Non-Verbal Scenario method was seen as an appropriate way of testing whether the sonic response to action made sense for the user. The participants found it easier to act without using actual words and with the help of props because, as several reported, they felt less embarrassed in front of the others.

Overall this workshop showed the benefits of using the embodied everyday experience as a point of departure in the participatory activities. Because the encounter with everyday sounds and objects is what we all share, even if it cannot be discussed in words - it can always be felt. Therefore, enacting an experience rather than solely observing and representing it, is at the core of the approach presented here.

Chapter 3
Sonic Interaction Design and its relation to film and theatre

Abstract How can the existing practices in theatre and cinema inform the design and evaluation of sonic interfaces? This question was addressed in a workshop held at the University of York in 2009. The whole process of designing the sounds for a short theatre scene, and directing and creating the final performance was experienced by a team of theatre professionals and sound designers, and it was finally exposed to the SID community.

3.1 Interactivity as performance

Interactivity has a lot to do with performance. This was recognized long ago to such extent that Brenda Laurel extended the theatre metaphor to include whole computer-based interactive systems [68], arguing that they are about (human or non-human) agents and actions, or representations of actions. In interaction design, the use of performative practices in the early stage of the design process is becoming increasingly popular. In bodystorming, contexts of use of interactive products are better understood by acting out as users or services [95]. Some scholars refer to embodied storming as the "art form" of bodystorming, and they claim that the experience of physical performance should come before ideation, just to enact experiential awareness [128].

At a more elaborate stage, the design process may use narrative and fictional strategies. This is particularly true for sonic interaction design, where the methods and techniques developed in the realm of fictional media can be readily adopted and further elaborated as soon as objects and services are put into a narrative context [56].

3.2 Structure of the workshop

The performing arts were considered as an additional field of practice and reflection in SID, both in the design process as well as in theoretical reflection. The workshop was structured to explore and exploit such field, as follows:

Narrative strategies, addressed through invited talks from film, game, and theatre sound experts, as well as trhough a call for sound designs for a theatrical scene;

Theatrical methods, used in the preparation and interpretation of the sonic interactions for the performed theatrical scene.

The workshop was organized in three stages: Call, Performance, and Evaluation.

3.3 The call for sound designs

The text of the theatrical scene "The New Anny", from the play "Attempts on Her Life" by Martin Crimp, was chosen as prompting material for sound designers. The scene describes several interactions with sounding objects, as well as many concepts and images that are open to a variety of interpretations. The style is that of a script for a car commercial, but the text builds up a tragic mood.

The sound designers were asked to submit two descriptions: (1) of each sound with actions or objects in the scene, and (2) of their interpretation, intentions, and technical strategies.

3.4 The performance

Two sound designs were selected for performance, representing two different approaches:

The sonic approach, followed by Stephen Barrass, focusing on the sounds of interactions with objects;

The musical approach, followed by Mary Luckhurst and Paul Abbott, based on their experience with sound design for theatre.

The actors were asked to rehearse the scene with the selected sound designs on the day before the workshop, largely using improvisation and interacting with the sound designer and the director Mary Luckhurst.

Fig. 3.1 Mark Smith performing

3.5 The evaluation

The audience was first exposed to the sound design in the dark, and their interpretations in terms of understanding of events, meanings of the sounds, expectations, and emotions were gathered and discussed. Then, the scene was performed by the actor and another discussion followed, especially focusing on the changes in perception and interpretation due to the performance. Finally, the sound designers were asked to compare their original intentions with the final realization and, with the help of director and actor, some conclusions on theatrical methods for SID were drawn.

3.6 Results

The results of the workshop, with special emphasis on the performance of Barrass' sound design, have been described in a publication [100]. The sound design was based in a kitchen environment, with substitutions of verb/noun pairs in the text with verb/nouns descriptors of kitchen sounds. However, the actual performance was given by a male actor (Mark Smith, figure 3.1) in a bathroom context, performing a sequence of actions and gestures that were arranged synchronously with the sound track. Consensus was reached in the audience (about thirty persons, mostly of the SID community) about the strong associations between sounds and synchronous actions, with radical changes in conveyed images when going from pure listening in the dark to listening while attending the performance. There were plausible and implausible associations which caused, respectively, reinforcement or surprise. In any case, a suspension of disbelieve made the audience trust the objects manipulated by the actor as the actual sources of sounds.

From theatre professionals, the process was described as innovative and liberating, as it gave more degrees of freedom to the performer, and it required an active interpretative process from the audience.

Interaction designers understood that sound designs must be put in a context of use to be actually evaluated. Theatre is a relatively complex testing experience, which makes more sense for problems that are inherently rich and articulated, although lightweight theatrical methods can be devised for more compact design problems [40]. It is clear that the actor and the audience have different perspectives and different degrees of involvement, and it is important that they would be both represented in a design team.

Chapter 4
Sketching Sonic Interaction Design

Abstract Sketching is an activity that is invariably present in the early stage of any design process. Unfortunately, sketching interactivity is not as immediate and effective as sketching the visual appearance of an object. For sketching sonic behaviors, however, the human voice is a powerful mean to produce sketches that facilitate the development of design ideas and the production of effective and aesthetically pleasing sounding objects.

4.1 Sketching interaction

Sketching is one of the most interesting research topics in interaction design [13]. As interaction is not easily captured by drawings, this activity is much different from traditional paper+pencil sketching of the visual aspect of objects. There are many ways to capture, mimic, or represent interaction, but none is nearly as effective as paper and pencil. That is why the interaction designers are so much interested in devising techniques and tools that can facilitate the sketching of interactive objects. Indeed, when the sonic behavior of objects is the focus of a design activity, humans do have a powerful sketching tool, which is their voice. Vocal imitations are commonly used to communicate the auditory aspect of objects, events, or processes.

The workshop organized in 2009 at the Holon Institute of Technology was a first initiative to explore sketching in sonic interaction design.

4.2 Structure of the workshop

The aim of this workshop was to bring together researchers of the SID community and practitioners in interaction design and other design fields, to discuss sonic sketching and the ideas of vocal sketching, and to experience firsthand a vocal sketching session as a starting point for a discussion on the value of this methodology. This has been a rare opportunity to experience, in one day, a combination of presentations and an actual, novel design activity, performed in multidisciplinary and multinational groups. There were thirtysix registered participants from thirteen countries at this workshop. In addition 4 helpers from the Faculty of Design, Holon, participated. The total number of participants was thus forty. The workshop programme included three invited speakers, six posters or demos presentations, and a group session of vocal sketching in which all participants worked in mixed groups on a two-hour experimental design task. The invited speakers, eminent scholars from the fields of music, design, and music technology, were Itay Talgam, conductor, Luka Or, designer, and Jordi Janer, music-technology researcher. Their presentations highlighted creative practices that can be transported across sectors. For example, the role of the orchestra conductor, as explained by Itay Talgam[1], could be effectively established in one of the vocal sketching sessions described in section 4.3.

All participants, including the invited speakers, participated to a joint exploration of vocal sketching.

4.3 Vocal sketching session

The voice is a tool that almost everybody have, and it is so immediate that it is often unconsciously used to mimic the sounds of animals, nature, and artifacts. In arranging a session on vocal sketching, the two main goals were:

design-centered exploration, of vocal sketching through three different design tasks;

process analysis, with special attention to inter-personal relations and social barriers.

The workshop was organized into three stages: warm-up, design, review.

---

[1] Itay Talgam on TED: http://www.ted.com/talks/itay_talgam_lead_like_the_great_conductors.html

| Power charger | Health vest | Water purifying bottle |

Fig. 4.1 Three design exercises on the theme of energy monitoring

Warm-up

A sonic guessing game was used to get the participants rapidly involved into group vocalization, confident of the possibilities that a combined use of voices have to represent complex sonic behaviors.

Design

Three physical object props were prepared (see figure 4.1): the "water-purifying bottle", the "energy-aware power charger", and the "health vest", each related to a class of signals and a form of energy – chemical, electrical, and physiological, respectively. The design task, for each of the six teams, was to create an interactive sound design for the prop it was assigned. Each team naturally and rapidly built up a narrative structure for the interaction, and was able to enact such interaction in front of a video camera, using vocal sketching to represent the sonic behavior of the designed objects.

Review

In the concluding session, after a shared viewing of some of the recorded videos, a discussion was open to exchange experiences and impressions, guided by the workshop leaders (I. Ekman and M. Rinott). A post-workshop questionnaire with fourteen open-ended questions was distributed to the participants, aimed at collecting information about previous experience, impressions on the achieved designs, design implications of vocal sketching, social comfort, and prospective developments.

4.4 Results

Five out of six teams were able to produce designs for two objects within one hour of sketching, including their enacted performance with the objects in front of the camera. This demonstrates the effectiveness of vocal sketching for sonic interaction design. This experience of enacting sonic interaction sketches in front of a camera adds up, with new means, to the experience gained in the previous workshop on theatrical sonic interaction design, described in chapter 3. Only a few of the participants were present in both workshops. Nevertheless, it seems that a common awareness of the possibilities of sound-centered bodystorming is now present in the SID community. This fact emerges from the collected answers to the questionnaire, that are analyzed in a publication by the workshop leaders and organizers [30].

Chapter 5
Human interaction with auditory displays

Abstract Interactive sonification is being used in some scientific fields to aid the exploration of large datasets or to precisely monitor physical processes and activities. Measures of efficiency must be combined with aesthetic criteria when evaluating auditory displays and interactive sonifications. A workshop and a journal special issue addressed these problems.

5.1 The workshop on Interactive Sonification

The third edition of the Interactive Sonification (ISon) workshop was co-organized by the COST Action on Sonic Interaction Design at KTH, Dept. of Speech Music and Hearing in Stockholm, Sweden, on April 7th 2010.

The workshop was organized as a single track including one keynote presentation, five long and six short paper presentations, four demonstrations, and six posters. The proceedings are freely available[1]. Here we only summarize the content of paper presentations, which give a glimpse of the field of interactive sonification as a whole. A post-workshop call for paper for a special issue of the Journal on Multimodal User Interfaces on Interactive Sonification resulted in twenty submissions. A description of such journal issue is given in section 5.6.

The keynote presentation "Listening to people, objects and interactions" was given by Tony Stockman, senior lecturer at the School of Electronic Engineering and

---

[1] http://www.interactive-sonification.org/ISon2010/proceedings/

Computer Science, Queen Mary University of London. In his presentation [132], Stockman examined a range of situations in which we experience the world through listening and gave hints about what can be taken into research of auditory displays. The everyday experience of visually-impaired persons is particularly interesting as a source of inspiration for effective uses of auditory displays.

5.2 Science and data exploration

Finding structures with a potential biological function within the many possible structures of an RNA sequence is a daunting task largely based on direct inspection. Sonification may be useful here if the structures are transformed into sonic gestalts in such a way that shape classes are immediately recognizable by ear. Grond et al. [49] followed such an approach, made effective by interactively manipulating both the visual and the auditory display during data exploration.

Growing Neural Gas is an algorithm that builds and grows a graph to reveal the dimensionality and structure of a data distribution. In [62] it is combined with model-based sonification to convey audible information about the distribution and to enable direct comparisons between distribution clusters. With multidimensional data, visualization by projection onto low-dimensional spaces may be complemented by active exploration of the structure: By "plucking" a neuron the structure resonates and provides auditory evidence of the neuron's neighborhood as well as of the whole network.

5.3 Sport and human movement

Interactive sonification, and in particular sonification of human gestures, is gaining much attention in sports science. Several experiments have been performed in different disciplines, and most of these present aspects of data acquisition, feature extraction, and acoustic representation through sound. Hummel et al. [57] presented the case of the German wheel, an apparatus made of two parallel rings connected by six bars. When using this object, the performer must be continuously aware of the orientation and speed of the wheel. Different kinds of sonification (direct, event-based, vowel, and cartoon rolling) were used, compared, and found to be differently effective for expert users.

The comparison of different sonification designs was also the kernel of the work of Barrass et al. [6], an intercontinental endeavor made possible by a collaboration between the Action on Sonic Interaction Design and the University of Canberra, supported by COST and the Australian Academy of Science (see section 15). In particular, the authors focused on streams of accelerometer data in the context of outdoor sports activities, and investigated different techniques and theories of sonification. They introduced a "technology probe" methodology in SID, which allows capturing the needs and desires of users in real-world setting, testing a technology, and getting inspirational ideas.

Among the sports that have attracted the attention of researchers in interactive sonification, rowing is among the most studied, probably because it is a complex optimization exercise involving human gesture, environmental conditions, and mental and physical fatigue. Schaffert et al. [125] explored auditory biofeedback as a mean to make elite German rowers aware of fine-grain temporal dynamics of movements. Listening to the boat motion, detailed information on the rowing cycle became intuitively comprehensible to the athletes and used to improve their performance. A similar project running in Sweden was presented by Dubus and Bresin [29]. Their aim was to enhance the training process so that it will converge faster and closer towards an optimal rowing technique. For this purpose, they were interested both in real-time monitoring and in a posteriori analysis by means of sonification. Their preliminary results showed that, although it is relatively easy to compare the sound patterns of beginners versus skilled rowers, the use of sonification with elite rowers makes other issues evident. For sustained training, an evaluation of the aesthetics and sustainability of auditory feedback is as important as its precision in rendering subtle temporal differences.

The European Project NIW (Natural Interactive Walking) has tight relations and a partial overlap with the interests of the Sonic Interacton Design community. It explores the possibilities for vibro-acoustic augmentation of shoes or floor tiles in walking or running. In [11] the relations between expressive intentions of walkers and different ground textures were investigated. The authors showed that harder textures lead to more aggressive walking patterns while softer textures lead to more tender walking styles. Different textures were rendered via interactive sound synthesis played through shoe-mounted loudspeakers. The Sound Design Toolkit [24] was used for sound synthesis.

5.4 Real and virtual environments

While computing devices are pervasively spreading in our everyday environment, it is increasingly important to find unobtrusive ways to communicate relevant in formation to humans. In this respect, audition is a privileged sense as it offers an always-open all-around monitoring channel. Bakker et al. [2] proposed some design cases exploring the possibilities of mechanically-generated informative sounds. They combined everyday physical interactions in the home with sounding objects that give peripheral awareness of ongoing events.

The creation of an immersive auditory display, as possible with wave field synthesis, affords spatial sorting of sonification streams. This approach, which merges spatial audio techniques with soundscape studies and multidimensional data sonification, was presented by Salvador [120].

21

5.5 Systems and frameworks

Sonification and vibrotactile feedback in objects and environments open new possibilities in interaction design. Großhauser and Hermann [50] provided a theoretical framework where different sonification modes (continuous vs. case-triggered), sensed variables (acceleration, orientation, distance, etc.), sound synthesis methods (additive, wavetable, physical modeling, etc.), and loudspeaker systems can be chosen to define an interactive closed-loop system. The approach was demonstrated through two design examples: An augmented drill, and a learning-tool for violin playing. Both these examples are aimed at augmenting human activities with effective sonic monitoring.

Another conceptual framework based on electroacoustic composition techniques was presented by Diniz et al. [26]. More precisely, interactive sonification is related with composition on one side, and with embodied music cognition on the other. As an example case, a system for the interactive exploration of one-dimensional datasets was coded and made accessible through a 3D visualization/navigation system, similar in spirit to Stockhausen's composition Mikrophonie I. This is a valuable example of how the visions of artists may inspire new approaches in science and technology.

5.6 A journal special issue

Roberto Bresin, Thomas Hermann and Andy Hunt launched a call for papers for a special issue on Interactive Sonification of the Journal on Multimodal User Interfaces (JMUI), in October 2010. The call was published in eight mailing lists in the field of Sound and Music Computing and on related websites. Twenty manuscripts were submitted for review, and eleven of them have been accepted for publication after further improvements. Two of the papers are further developments of works presented at ISon 2010.

The papers give an interesting overview of the field of Interactive Sonification as it is today. Their topics include the sonification of motion and of data exploration, a new sound synthesis model suitable for interactive sonification applications, a study on perception in the everyday periphery of attention, and the proposal of a conceptual framework for interactive sonification.

Motion

One of the papers presents a follow-up study of work presented at ISon 2010 [29]. In this work authors present an evaluation of four sound models for the sonification of elite rowing. The sonified data were those of the movement (speed and acceleration) of a single scull rowing boat. Results show a good ability of athletes to efficiently extract basic characteristics of the sonified data, and highlight the important issue of aesthetics in interactive sonification design. In another paper dedicated to motion, authors present three interactive sonification models of the synchronisation of gestures between two people each shaking a mobile phone. Interactive sonification of their hand movements helped users to keep synchronized with each other. In a study on the sonification of everyday actions, e.g., pressing a button on an ATM machine, researchers found that the level of usability (low vs. high) of the user interface affects the choice of sounds that best deliver a sense of naturalness of the interaction.

Data exploration

This is the traditional topic of Interactive Sonification, and is reflected by the number of papers in this category, five out of eleven. In an interesting study the authors apply voice synthesis (vowel sounds) for the sonification of mathematical functions. In another work, the authors discuss the interaction design for tabletop computing for exploring and interacting with representations of time-series data simultaneously in both the visual and auditory modalities. Authors of another manuscript focusing on data exploration present an approach to designing hierarchy-based sonification for supporting non-visual interaction with relational diagrams. In another study authors propose the use of a multimodal tangible interface that allows the users to explore data in both time and space dimensions while receiving immediate sonic feedback of their actions. This interface is applied to phenology, the study of periodic biological processes, and can be used to explore the effects of climate change. Sonification of the environment for delivering location-based information to mobile users is the challenge faced by another research work focusing on the sonification of data. The system allows for increased awareness of the environment for users with limited vision capabilities or whose visual attention is otherwise occupied in other tasks.

Sound synthesis

In an original work authors present a physics-based sound synthesis model of liquid phenomena suitable for interactive sonification. In fact the representation of continuous processes in interaction and interface design often uses liquid metaphors, such as dripping or streaming of fluids.

Perception

In a follow-up study of their work presented at ISon 2010 [2] the authors present a qualitative study on the everyday periphery of attention. They found that sound plays a major role, supporting their approach to use interactive sonification as an interaction style for peripheral interaction.

Conceptual framework

In a further development of their study presented at ISon 2010 [26], Diniz et al. present in more detail their theoretical foundations combining gestalt-based electroacoustic composition techniques, user body-centered spatial exploration and mediation technology for the definition of a conceptual framework for interactive sonification.

Part II
Training Schools

Chapter 6
Biomedical data sonification

Abstract The Training School on Biomedical Data Sonification was the first training programme of the COST Action on Sonic Interaction Design, organised with the goal of promoting interdisciplinary education and research in the fields of sonification, datamining, sound computing and SID. The thematic focus was on sonification, the systematic representation of data as sound, and on how sonification can support the understanding of patterns in complex data. The programme provided insights and inspiration from a multi-faceted emerging field, including data analysis, sonification, bio-medical applications, sound studies and sound art.

6.1 Sonification in science

Biomedical data exploration is one of the scientific activities where sonification may prove to be useful to support research, practices and data analysis. To investigate these possibilities, a Training School on Biomedical Data Sonification was organized by Thomas Hermann in Bielefeld, on February 2008[1].

Twentynine attendees from seven European countries used the three-days training school to share ideas. A densely packed program of courses and presentations, discussions and practical hands-on sessions provided inspiration for research directions that were further explored in the COST Action on Sonic Interaction Design.

---

[1] http://www.cost-sid.org/wiki/SIDTrainingSchool200802

The Geiger counter, as a tool for sonification of ionizing radiation, is often cited as a prominent example of how nuclear physics may meet sound. It has been used for over a century in several application fields, including geophysics and medical therapy. In the history of medicine, the stethoscope is known to have radically changed, upon its introduction in the first half on nineteenth century, the relation between doctor and patient and the whole practice of diagnosis in medicine [131] . With the stethoscope, auscultation became an examination practice mediated by an instrument, and based on listening skills developed by medical students. In a sense, both the Geiger counter and the stethoscope afford a sort of interactive sonification, where the tool is used to explore a space through sound.

Modern sonification offers much more complex and refined methods to turn data into audible sound, making it possible to understand temporal, spectral and spatial features in appropriately organized multivariate time-series such as EEG, or to render meaningful auditory representations even for data that lack any time attribute, as for instance in data sets where the measurements characterize different features of biological probes.

While visualization is an important and established means to investigate such biomedical data sets, the TS addressed the question how sonification can complement visual inspection, or even replace it so that the visual sense is set free for other activities. For instance, in EEG monitoring, the online sonification can enable clinicians to observe and interact with the patient while simultaneously staying informed about the real-time EEG measurements. In classical information systems, however, the same task demands alternatively looking at the patient and at the visual display.

The starting point for TS was therefore an overview of the different existing approaches of sonification in the biomedical field, presented according to the application type (probing, interactive sonification, process monitoring, rapid summary, data exploration). The discussed applications ranged from MRI sonification, tissue sonification over proteomics, support for surgical navigation to ECG and EEG sonification, including also related topics such as the sonification of verbatim psychotherapy session protocols. In summary, this gave an idea of the breadth of possible applications of sonification.

A particular challenge is, however to understand high-dimensional structures by using sound. Therefore the following necessary step was to give a condensed course on data mining techniques including methods for dimensionality reduction and neural computation. The take home message was that the available methods are already quite powerful to explain coarse structures of data distributions such as clustering, linear dependencies, etc., and sonification can maybe contribute best by focusing on the less apparent patterns such as rhythmical organization, or hidden regularities in the residuals.

As a third step, the TS provided a review of the different sonification techniques (audification, parameter-mapping sonification, earcons and auditory icons, model-based sonification), to understand where and how they can support the data analysis process.

Invited lectures allowed to set a focus on specific techniques and applications. Eoin Brazil reported on the utility of Auditory Icons for notifications in the operation theatre. Gerold Baier reviewed the history of listening in medicine, from auscultation and the stethoscope to the modern listening practices in EEG sonification. A specific complementary view was brought in by a session on art and science, where the focus was to look at how biosignals have been used in artistic contexts (presentation by Jean-Julien Filatriau). A focus on EEG signals for musical performances was brought in by Andrew Brouse and Cumhur Erkut who reported in an invited lecture on the physiological interfaces developed in the eNTERFACE' 07 workshop [31].

The third day of the workshop gave more opportunities for individual hands-on experiences. Till Bovermann gave a practical course on "Sonification with Super-Collider", Florian Grond showed interactively how sonification has been applied to problems in chemistry, and Matthias Rath discussed the relation of interactive sonification to physical models. An inspiring perspective on the topic was finally brought in by the invited lecture "On Functional Sounds" by Georg Spehr, where functions of sound were expanded beyond the information purpose, and context and situation were acknowledged.

The Training School aimed at expanding the horizon of interactive sonification to include areas of biomedicine where sound is not yet considered as a powerful tool for making data immediately perceivable. The programme was advertised also to local Bielefeld students in computer science who were previously exposed to sound synthesis fundamentals, forming a good team with mixed expertise that included domain experts, SID experts, sonification experts and programming-skilled people.

In summary, as seen from the organizer, invited lecturers and attendees, the training school was very inspiring and provided relevant new information for the attendees with their heterogeneous backgrounds. The sessions always ended in very alive discussions during the coffee breaks and at the end different new connections between European partners have been established and strengthened.

6.2 Training School programme

- **Biomedical data sonification - Overview**
  - Introduction and sonification overview (Thomas Hermann)
  - Auditory icons for notifications - Medical devices and sounds in the operation theatre (Eoin Brazil)

- **Data and techniques**
  - Data mining techniques for biomedical data (Thomas Hermann)
  - Sonification techniques - An overview (Thomas Hermann)
  - Listening in medicine - A historical review (Gerold Baier)

- **Sonification and EEG**
  - Application focus: Human EEG (Gerold Baier)

  - Sonification techniques for human EEG data (Thomas Hermann and Gerold Baier)

- **Art and science**

  - Introduction on the use of biosignals in artistic contexts (Jean-Julien Filatriau)
  - EEG/Biosignals controlled musical performance (Andrew Brouse)
  - SID with physiological interfaces in the eNTERFACE-07 workshop (Cumhur Erkut)
  - Poster presentations by the participating students

- **Practical hands-on session and perspectives session**

  - SuperCollider - A practical course (Till Bovermann)
  - Hands-on session
  - Sonification in chemistry (Florian Grond)
  - Interactive sonification and physical models (Matthias Rath)
  - On functional sounds (Georg Spehr)

- **Panel Discussion: Perspectives for biomedical data sonification**
- **Summary and conclusion**

Chapter 7
Interacting with urban sounds

Abstract In 2009 the conference on Sound and Music Computing was held in Porto. A Training School and an Inspirational Session on Sonic Interaction Design were organized, where the focus was on interaction through and with the sounds of the environment, at both a urban and a personal scale.

7.1 Urban soundscapes

The topic of urban soundscapes and their relation with mobile technologies has been explored by the COST Action on Sonic Interaction Design, both through Short-Term Scientific Missions (see section 15.2) and through a Training School that was held in Porto in july 2009, right before the Conference on Sound and Music Computing.

The theme of the TS was "Interacting with Sounds of Porto" and the aim was to guide students to explore the potential of recording, processing, sharing and interacting with city sounds. This School aimed at giving an opportunity to young researchers interested in the field of Sound and Music Computing to showcase their ideas, learn new skills and work with senior researchers. During four days, the program included lectures and hands-on practical sessions under the supervision of tutors who provided one-to-one mentoring on artistic and/or scientific projects focused on interactions with sounds that reflect the city of Porto and its activities.

The School included three main lectures:

1. Design of new interfaces for musical expression (Marcelo Wanderley, Input Devices and Music Interaction Laboratory - CIRMMT - Schulich School of Music, McGill University). This lecture reviewed existing examples of novel interfaces for musical expression (also known as gestural controllers or control surfaces), as well as the various sensing technologies used in these devices. It also discussed ways to design mapping strategies between interface output variables and sound synthesis input variables, and approaches to the design of novel interfaces and digital musical instruments.
2. Registering the soundscape (Joel Chadabe, Electronic Music Foundation). This lecture presented aesthetic, technical, and cultural aspects of audio field recording, interactive approaches to sound design with environmental sounds, and the nature of the roles that soundscape composition can play in our lives.
3. Sound edition, description and retrieval, and social networks (Xavier Serra, Music Technology Group, Universitat Pompeu Fabra). This lecture presented current technologies for sound edition, description and retrieval, and introduced students to the use of the `Freesound.org` platform with which they then edited, tagged and shared their sound recordings.

The tutors were:

- Emilia Gómez (Universitat Pompeu Fabra, Barcelona)
- Fabien Gouyon (INESC Porto, COST SID MC Member)
- Stephan Baumann (German Research Center for AI)
- Eoin Brazil (University of Limerick)
- Bram de Jong (Freesound project)
- Luis Gustavo Martins (Universidade Católica, Porto)
- Rui Penha (Casa da Música, Porto)
- Stefania Serafin (Aalborg University, Copenhagen)
- Federico Fontana (University of Verona)

Twentyone students were selected from fiftysix candidates from twelve different countries. One of the criteria for recruitment was to have a good assortment of backgrounds, including art, audio engineering, design, computer science, etc.. This allowed effective science-art cross-fertilization.

The venue for lectures and hands-on session was particularly remarkable. It was the Casa da Musica, designed by Rem Koolhaas, opened in 2005 and now a major city landmark. Besides being a large concert hall, Casa da Musica hosts Digitòpia, a platform for the development of digital music communities.

Students walked around the city of Porto, and could geo-reference their recordings through GPS datalogging. The recorded signals were directly captured in the audible range or taken from inaudible bands (Gigahertz of wireless networks and ultrasounds) and made audible through frequency shifting. Then, in the hands-on session these recordings were made accessible through audible maps, micro-controller based circuits, and Wiimote controllers.

One of the prototypes, calles Portification, consisted of five force-sensitive resistors (FSR) and two ribbon sensors that were glued on an alternative map of Porto and a webcam that was placed above the map. For each FSR the audience could trigger three sounds (recorded at the same location) depending on the amount of pressure exerted. For each ribbon sensor five sounds could be triggered depending on the position of the finger on the ribbon. The webcam tracked the movement from the audience when they moved from one sensor to another and the sound evolved depending on that position.

Another project, called Andante, provided a multiangled soundwalking of Porto, made accessible through Wiimote controllers[1].

Aftereffects of a Training School

The experience gained by participants of the TS was exploited in some artistic and scientific works that were realized afterwards. Among these, we mention:

- Participant Cléo Palacio-Quintin made a one-minute composition for piano, video, and sounds recorded during the TS[2]. The piece was premiered at the Chapelle historique du Bon-Pasteur in Montréal, on October 2009;
- One paper presented at the International Conference on Auditory Display (ICAD 2010) was inspired by the work done by João Cordeiro during the TS [19]. In the TS project "Casa dos Aliens" a number of students, including Cordeiro, worked under the guidance of Eoin Brazil.
- Participant Lisa Kori Chung used the field recordings from Portugal in a binaural sound installation that was included in the senior show for her undergraduate degree at Oberlin Conservatory. The recordings were triggered based on the x,y location of the listener. The environment is shown in figure 7.1. Chung also received a grant for a year (July 2010-August 2011) of research and traveling through the world of electronic art, to compare and contrast different technologically-based art practices in varying cultural contexts[3]. She started writing the grant application during the TS, having great help from discussions with other participants and teachers.
- Participant Daniele Salvati wrote a number of papers in continuation of the work done during the TS on browsable soundscapes [121, 122, 14].

7.2 Interactive sounds in everyday life

The Sound and Music Computing Conference included a special track on Sonic Interaction Design and an Inspirational Session chaired by Karmen Franinovic.

Some evocative scenarios were presented to elicit the imagination of the Inspirational Session attendees:

---

[1] http://vimeo.com/5856976

[2] http://vimeo.com/7578909

[3] http://themediumandthemayhem.net

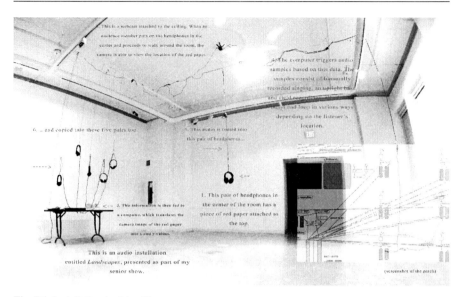

Fig. 7.1 Installation by Lisa Chung

An alarm clock that you cannot hear, but still wakes you up. A shower curtain that sings along with you. Chewing gum that allows you to catch sounds that surround you and chew them into a new remixed soundscape. An umbrella that creates your personal acoustic shield. A pair of gloves that can catch the sounds, mould and sculpt them like clay... What will our interactive future sound like? What do you think the sonic world should or will become? What are you making or imagining that can be a part of this world?

Discussion was stimulated by the following short presentations of scenarios and prototype realizations:

- Daniel Hug "The Wise Bathroom: A personal place of cleansing, insight and truth";
- Federico Fontana, Stefano Papetti and Marco Civolani "A sonic shoe for ecological ground augmentation";
- Alain Crevoisier "Sonic interaction on the Playroom table";
- Sylvain Le Groux "Towards emotion-driven interactive sound design: Bridging the gaps between affect, physiology and sound generation";
- Daniel Bisig "SoL: artificial grass that confers an acoustic memory";
- Martin Rumori "Enactive Soundscape Browsing in Binaural Audio Augmented Environments";
- Willow Tyrer "Accent GPS";
- Robert Annies, Kamil Adiloglu, Hendrik Purwins "Playing with Sonic Interaction Design"

Chapter 8
Product sound design

Abstract Product designers, engineers, artists, and business planners adopt practices and approaches that seem distinct, when not even diverging. A common interest can be the key for making them cooperate, and such interdisciplinary collaboration can spur true innovation. That is what happened at the Training School held in Helsinki in 2010, where a set of trainees with a variety of backgrounds were put to work together around the common interest in interactive sound.

8.1 The product design process

Prominent interaction design experts claim that the development of a literacy on understanding, interpreting, and collecting a repertoire of sketches and prototypes is a core issue in interaction design [5, 73, 77]. Designing for manipulative interaction requires a shift of attention from the product itself towards interaction. Designers need tools and techniques to explore, visualize, interpret, and refine interaction. Research and education, through shared practices of creation, manipulation, and interpretation, are aimed at exploiting the richness and expressiveness of movement, of both users and objects.

In SID, there is a growing corpus of knowledge on sound to be exploited in interaction design activities [10, 30, 39, 56, 24, 114]. The development of such a literacy represents a crucial step towards the education of product design team members with a specific competence on interactive sound. Since 2008, the COST Action on Sonic Interaction Design organized (see chapters 6 and 7) several training activities devoted to the creation and consolidation of this innovative and interdisciplinary domain. In particular, the Summer School on Product Sound Design was held in August 2010, under the organization of Cumhur Erkut, Stefano Delle Monache, and Daniel Hug, and it was developed along two main principles:

1. to start an integration process of product sound design with product development and design;
2. to bring together the state of the art of the several tools, techniques and interdisciplinary guidelines that are constantly under development and investigation in the SID community.

The summer school was positioned at the intersection between product design and sonic interaction design: problem-based learning activities – that involve ideas to realize and problems to solve by planning, searching for information, decision making, manufacturing, assembling and testing – were merged with sonic activities, such as making designers sensitive to sonic interactions by means of soundwalks, by analyzing and imitating sonic gestures, and by sonic explorations devoted to concept development, sound sketching and scenario enactment.

For this purpose, two partnering companies, *Hipui*[1] and *Powerkiss*[2], were involved in order to provide participants with a real scenario to be confronted with. For the summer school, Hipui was interested in exploring the use of non-verbal sound to support the execution of gestural input in handheld and eyes-free devices. Powerkiss' open problem was in auditory signalling their wireless charging technology, so that the latter could be invisible and merge completely with the host artifact, a table for instance. Sonic branding aspects and context of use, private or public, had to be considered.

In figure 8.1, the proposed design themes frame the contents of the whole training activities.

8.2 Four days of research through design

Day One

The first day was devoted to provide some basic skills and tools aimed at being sensitized to sound in interaction, at collecting and enacting fast and rough ideas, and at generating quick and dirty sonic prototypes:

- Soundwalk and listening session (Frauke Behrendt): it encompasses a series of listening and sound walking exercises, aimed at sensitizing to sonic interactions, improving listening skills, expanding the vocabulary to talk about sounds, representing visually and orally the temporal, spatial, embodied aspects of sound [146];

---

[1] http://www.hipui.com/
[2] http://www.powerkiss.com/

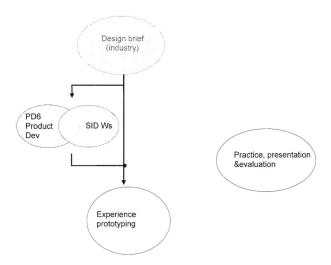

Fig. 8.1 The structure of the Summer School

- Vocal sketching session (Inger Ekman): it introduces the use of vocal sounds as means for rapid sonic prototyping of design ideas, especially in the early stage of the design process. Groups were asked to use their voice to sketch the sonic behaviour of a given artifact [30] (see also chapter 4);
- PD6 - product development in 6 hours (Wycliffe Raduma): it is a workshop format developed at Design Factory, Helsinki. Prototyping and hands-on are at the center of a non-linear, iterative process of planning, concept development, design, testing and refinement [110, 111].

Day Two

The second day was dedicated to provide analytical tools for concept development and to experiment with various sound making techniques for sonic prototyping:

- Narration and performativity in sonic interactive commodities (Daniel Hug): this session provided analytical tools for interpreting and developing narratives around sound, starting from a systematic analysis of film or game sound cases [56] (see also chapters 3 and 13);
- Sound - from perception to basic design (Stefano Delle Monache): this session introduced an analytical/synthetic approach to sound in continuous and multi-sensory interaction. Participants were asked to prototype the sonic interaction by manipulating some sound models, available in the Sound Design Toolkit, a physics-based sound generation application [24, 114].

Days Three and Four

Days three and four were dedicated to independent work of the groups. The briefs given for the PD6 workshop were refined and better specified according to the indications coming from the participating companies:

- Powerkiss: Create a system that makes wireless charging intuitive, easy and informative. Extend your device for social information sharing;
- Hipui: Make an interactive alternative for a display and keyboard/touch interface. Extend your device for information navigation;
- Requirements for both: Feedback and interaction are handled by the use of non-verbal sound and gestures. Demonstrate the discovery of functions and capabilities in an extreme situation with experience prototyping.

8.3 Evaluation

Fiftysix applications to the School were received from all over the world. They were classified as coming from engineering (39%), design (36%), economics (9%), and music (16%). Compared to previous educational activities organized by the COST Action on Sonic Interaction Design, the applicants profile was much more design- and less science- or art-oriented. Conversely, almost nobody had specific skills on SID.

The workshop modules were constructed in order to ensure a ratio of 80-90% of practice and 20-10% of related contact teaching, with intensive training on sound methods and techniques concentrated in the early stage.

After completing the summer school, students were asked to evaluate, in a feedback form, the workshops, the instructors, their experience of the training activities, and participation to groups work. The activities and the various perspectives on SID, though condensed in two very intensive, and sometimes hectic, days, were almost unanimously evaluated useful learning experiences, with a high degree of applicability to own work. Considered the multidisciplinary background of the participants, and the different levels of access, such a result confirms a value and trust in the tools and techniques that are being investigated in the Sonic Interaction Design community.

As seen from the instructors, tutors, and evaluators, the school was a great source of inspiration. It was understood that giving much details about software tools diverts the attention from the design aspects of sound in interaction. It was recognized that the diverse backgrounds that were initially mixed in all groups are actually needed to develop good product sound design, and that a common platform for effective team work can be found. The problems and hints given by the partner companies were at the same time concrete and broad and they elicited a number of research questions that are still animating the community.

Part III
Short-Term Scientific Missions

Chapter 9
Sound synthesis

Abstract Sound synthesis is at the heart of any auditory display or interactive sonification. Devising methods and techniques that are computationally and perceptually effective is, therefore, of prominent interest for Sonic Interaction Design. The field of sound synthesis has been advanced through a series of collaborations among some of the most active laboratories. Physical modeling, in particular, is of much interest as a family of sound synthesis methods that provide highly-controllable sound models.

9.1 Physical modeling

Although in Sonic Interaction Design the sound of traditional musical instruments is only occasionally coupled to information or to human action, the knowledge and understanding being developed in the field of musical acoustics can provide important reference points.

Heidi-Maria Lehtonen recently completed her Ph.D. at Aalto University on analysis and modeling of piano sounds [69]. Her studies benefited from two research missions, one held at KTH, Stockholm, and the other held at the University of Verona. Both missions were aimed at investigating the subtle nuances of piano timbre that can be introduced by the interactive control of dampers. At KTH Lehtonen collected some high-quality recordings of piano tones played with different degrees of sustain pedaling. Then, she designed an experiment to assess how perceivable is the half-pedaling effect, and she started looking at possible ways to incorporate such effect into real-time sound synthesis. The analysis of the recorded sounds led to a journal publication [70]. At the University of Verona, the attention was mostly focused on how to efficiently recreate the pedaling effect, and some working solutions have been developed [148]. In fact, the collaboration between Aalto and Verona Universities was truly bidirectional, as Ph.D. candidate Stefano Zambon was also recipient of a grant for a Short-Term Scientific Mission in Helsinki. While the Italian group has been developing a piano model based on modal synthesis [4], the Finnish researchers mainly used robust signal-processing algorithms. The collaboration helped advancing the state of the art in piano modeling, with positive side effects for non-musical sound synthesis. For example, the calibration algorithm of the pedal effect can be used to extract modal parameters from coupled systems with a high modal density. This kind of estimation is often useful in relating physical models of sounding objects to recorded sounds.

The collaboration between Aalto and Verona Universities was further strengthened through two other missions that gave important methodological and theoretical contributions to physics-based sound synthesis. Balázs Bank developed a method for measuring and synthesizing passive admittance matrices. The reference case is still in musical acoustics [3], but his model is useful in the block-based modeling of general sounding objects, since all vibrating bodies can be described by admittance matrices. Using passive model blocks and connecting them by wave variables results in inherently stable sound models. That is, the sound designer does not have to worry about stability issues and has a complete flexibility in the connection and parameterization of the models. Similar signal-processing concerns were shared by Federico Fontana, who contributed a processing framework for the continuous control of sound synthesis. Since the beginning of the COST Action on Sonic Interaction Design, continuous interaction and multisensory feedback have been found to be a fertile ground for research and experimentation (see section 1). One of the basic problems for sound synthesis in these contexts is how to build networks of nonlinear filters that afford interactive and continuous manipulation of their parameters. Again, musical instruments were used as complex reference cases [17, 38], but the methods generalize to non-musical sound synthesis as well. Fontana's mission at Helsinki attracted much interest from several researchers and nurtured a six-month postdoc internship, funded by the Academy of Finland, by Jyri Pakarinen from Aalto University to the University of Verona. Furthermore, two journal special issues were eventually released [97, 141].

9.2 Contact sounds

A site where sound synthesis for interactive applications is being advanced is the Medialogy Department at Aalborg University Copenhagen. Stefano Papetti used his mission at Medialogy to investigate possible extensions of the palette of sound models currently available in the Sound Design Toolkit [24]. His Ph.D. dissertation [98], defended in 2010, focuses on robust and accurate synthesis of everyday sounds. In particular, contact sounds are made of elementary impact events and friction processes, and it is important to look for well-behaved numerical methods for such elementary phenomena [99]. A research project that involves both the Universities of Verona and Aalborg at Copenhagen is NIW (Natural Interactive Walking[1]), where contact sounds are extensively used in floor interfaces and augmented shoes.

One of the contact phenomena that are most relevant for continuous interaction is rolling. Mathieu Lagrange from McGill University visited INESC Porto to develop a new synthesis model for rolling, to be used with an original haptic device, called the T-STICK. Lagrange proposed an excitation+resonance approach to sound synthesis, where the pseudo-random generation of pulses is made to depend on tilt of the stick. This analysis/synthesis method was later published in a journal [65]. As a final result of his mission in Porto, Lagrange implemented an audio-haptic installation for the Digitòpia project of Casa da Musica (see chapter 7).

It is interesting to notice that, in a few years, rolling has become a fertile simulation playground in sound and haptic synthesis, with at least four independent and perceptually-validated realizations [65, 109, 133, 147]. One of these realization is the one by Matthias Rath, often associated with a physical device called the Ballancer [109]. As a researcher at Deutsche Telekom Laboratories, Rath developed his device and synthesis method, and in a visit at IRCAM-Paris he had a chance to compare the Ballancer with another abstract sonic interactive device, the Spinotron [71] (see also chapter 1). This comparison also extends to two sound synthesis approaches to physical modeling, one based on explicit laws of interaction force, and now incorporated in the Sound Design Toolkit [24], and the other based on geometrical constraints of contact, and implemented in the Modalys software by IRCAM [7].

9.3 Control of synthesizers

While with sound synthesis by physical modeling the problem of control is recast as manipulation of objects according to the laws of physics, for all other synthesis methods the setting and control of parameters is as important as the synthesis algorithm.

James McDermott has been proposing various evolutionary-programming techniques to help musicians and sound designers to deal effectively with the parameter-control problem [81]. In his visit to Chalmers University, McDermott designed and tested a system based on the musical keyboard (as a familiar control space) and on neural networks that generalize from well-behaved mappings.

Julien Castet, in a collaboration with Jean-Julien Filatriau at Université Catholique de Louvain, experimented on a fluid-dynamic simulation for controlling the synthesis of textural sounds, as obtained through granular or concatenative sound synthesis. As an application, the "People are sounds" installation has been conceived. It is

---

[1] `http://www.niwproject.eu`

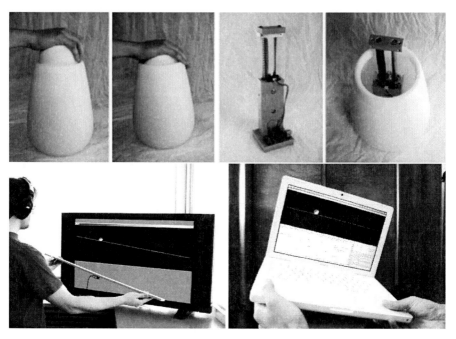

Fig. 9.1 The Spinotron (top) and the Ballancer (bottom, two realizations)

based on a video capture of human activities in a crowded environment, and it offers a new perception of interpersonal relationships within a local group, as if they were sonic manifestations of fluids in motion.

Two of the strongest research groups working on the problems of sound-synthesis control and mapping of gestures to synthesis parameters are found at the Real-Time Musical Interactions team at IRCAM-Paris and at the CIRMMT centre of McGill University. Tommaso Bianco established a collaboration between the two institutions on the topic of gesture coarticulation (a subject widely studied in phonetics) in sound production. This topic is particularly important for those sound-generating phenomena that are largely based on the human body. One prominent example is oscillations of lip reeds, as in trumpet playing, where the respiratory and oral systems cooperate to determine the time evolution of control parameters. Here, pressure, force, and electromyographic sensors were used to measure the control signals [9]. The interesting question addressed by Bianco was if and how these control functions could translate to different control modalities, for example using a lever instead of a mouthpiece. This translation is likely to be possible at the coarticulation level, regardless of particular musical skills, thus being helpful in the design of sonic interactive products, especially those involving tight, continuous, and adaptive mapping.

Chapter 10
Sound analysis and organization

Abstract Abstracting sounds, extracting features, and segregating auditory objects are all activities that enable, in a human-machine interaction loop, the stages of processing, synthesis, and decision making. Organizing sonic interactions in browsable spaces helps the designer looking for inspirational patterns or reference cases.

10.1 Auditory scene analysis

Computational Auditory Scene Analysis (CASA) aims at identifying and grouping the perceived sound objects in auditory streams [145]. Marsyas is an open source software framework [140] that is popular among researchers in Music Information Retrieval (MIR) and that has recently been used to implement some preliminary work in the field of CASA [64, 79].

Two of the active developers of Marsyas, Luis Gustavo Martins and Mathieu Lagrange, exploited a Short-Term Scientific Mission to further develop a system for sound-object segregation in complex sound mixtures by using sinusoidal modeling and by clustering spectral peaks based on cues inspired on the current knowledge of how the human auditory system analyses music mixtures (see figure 10.1). In their implementation, the analysis is fully bottom up and the system does not require previous training nor makes use of previous knowledge of sound models, being mainly based on the definition of perceptual cues to group spectral components in a time-frequency representation of the mixture signal. The objective is for the system to

be able to segregate sound objects in the mixture with a close perceptual corre-
spondence to the sound objects as they are perceived by a human listener. Martins,
Lagrange, and Marsyas initiator George Tzanetakis published a description of this
tool in a book chapter [80].

The approach to soundscape analysis proposed by Ming Yang starts from the
assumption that music could be regarded as an imitation of environmental soundscapes, or as an ideal soundscape of the mind. In a STSM in Porto she applied music
information retrieval (MIR) software packages, including Marsyas, to the analysis
of environmental sounds. The extracted musical features (harmony, pitch, rhythm,
etc.) can be used to describe different soundscapes. Ming Yang's STSM can be
regarded as a scientific cross-fertilization between the COST Action on Sonic Interaction Design and the COST Action on the Soundscape of European Cities and
Landscapes[1].

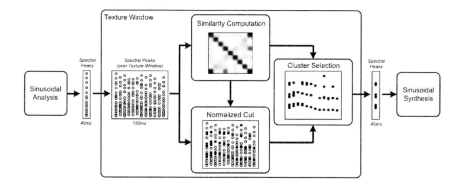

Fig. 10.1 Block-diagram for a sound-object segregation framework

10.2 Composite audio analysis and synthesis

The COST Action on Sonic Interaction Design contributed to the realization of the
project Audiogarden in a long-term research program (NUMEDIART) centered on
Digital Media Arts, funded by the Région Wallonne, Belgium[2]. This was possible through a Short-Term Scientific Mission of Cécile Picard from INRIA Sophia
Antipolis (France) to Université de Mons (Belgium). The Audiogarden project is
aimed at sound composers and designers, and it provides a tool that combines hypermedia navigation with interactive sound synthesis, with special focus on sound
textures [102]. This realization required the development of three blocks:

---

[1] COST Action TC0804: http://soundscape-cost.org/
[2] http://www.numediart.org

- Automatic analysis of audio recordings. Extraction and classification of meaningful audio grains;
- Automatic synthesis of coherent soundtracks based on the arrangement of audio grains in time;
- Interface for audio database manipulation and sound composition, with special attention to browsable visualizations of sound collections (see figure 10.2).

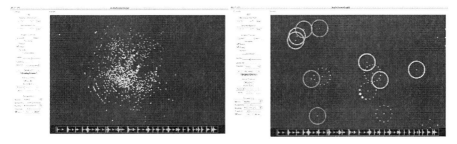

Fig. 10.2 Two alternative visualizations, both featuring a two-pane view: audio database browser by similarity (top), waveform of the sound being synthesized (bottom).

10.3 Organizing sonic interactions

The organization of sonic interaction and the construction of a Sonic Interaction Atlas [54] has been one of the goals of the COST Action on Sonic Interaction Design since its early activities (see chapter 1). A taxonomy has been developed in order to catch the structural differences of sonic interactions along five major lines: subject, object, action, perceptions, and action-perception loop (see table 10.1). A graphical application has been written, using the `SuperCollider` language, to enter and edit sonic interaction examples, and to generate a numerical representation to be used in other utilities.

Thomas Hermann applied multidimensional scaling to the numeric representation of sonic interaction examples to compute a two-dimensional map, which represents the Sonic Interaction Atlas. Figure 10.3 shows a screenshot where an adapted map is visible on the right side. The most common use case of the sonic interaction atlas will be to search for inspiration on how to accompany an interaction with sound. In this case, some attributes may already be given by the interaction at hand. In this case, the already known attributes can be specified in the query window shown in figure 10.3 on the left side, leaving all unknown attributes on the setting "unclear". Real-time adaptation moves to the points of the map where inspiring examples can possibly be found.

user characterization	use_finger, use_hand, use_foot, use_tool, task_chgworld, task_query, task_none, task_monitor
object characterization	obj_dof_binary, obj_dof_1d, obj_dof_2d, obj_dof_nd, obj_rigid, obj_fluid, obj_gas, obj_malleable, obj_elastic, obj_distributed
action type and action	acty_discrete, acty_continuous, acty_reversible, acty_sequenced, act_contact, act_shake, act_scrub, act_squeeze, act_shape, act_pluck, act_move, act_rotate
perceptual channels	per_sound, per_vision, per_haptics, per_temp
context	seq_elementary, seq_compound, loo_discrete, loo_continuous, loo_selfctrl

Table 10.1 Binary attributes used to characterize sonic interactions

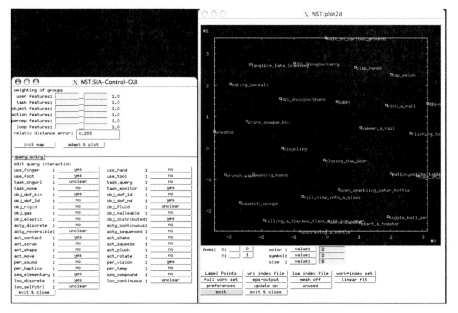

Fig. 10.3 The Sonic Interaction Atlas

New applications and challenges for interactive sonification were presented in a keynote speech [51] by Hermann at the Conference on Digital Audio Effects (DAFx) in Graz, Austria.

A STSM by Eoin Brazil to IRCAM-Paris was dedicated to the organization of sound taxonomies for the purpose of constructing a design space. The understanding of a taxonomy does not necessarily lead to a good design solution, but it can help informing the designer's choices. His review of methods and framework for SID led to an extensive survey of existing approaches [10]. Figure 10.4 highlights some of the most relevant existing design approaches, and Figure 10.5 summarizes the key features of existing sound perception taxonomies that are relevant for SID.

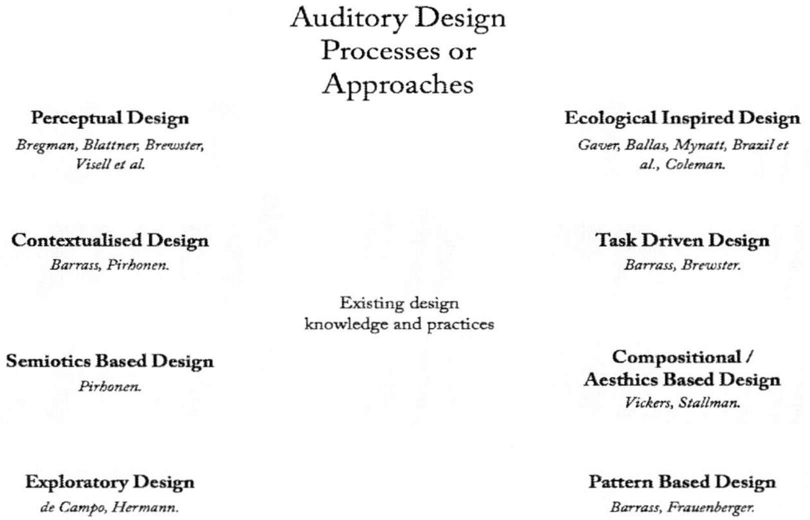

Auditory Design
Processes or
Approaches

Perceptual Design
*Bregman, Blattner, Brewster,
Visell et al.*

Ecological Inspired Design
*Gaver, Ballas, Mynatt, Brazil et
al., Coleman.*

Contextualised Design
Barrass, Pirhonen.

Task Driven Design
Barrass, Brewster.

Existing design
knowledge and practices

Semiotics Based Design
Pirhonen.

**Compositional /
Aesthics Based Design**
Vickers, Stallman.

Exploratory Design
de Campo, Hermann.

Pattern Based Design
Barrass, Frauenberger.

Fig. 10.4 A selection of existing design approaches

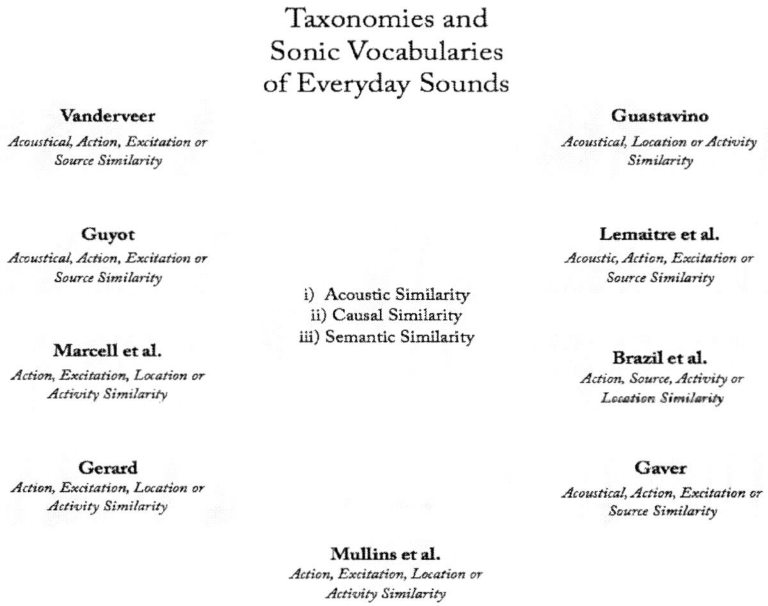

Taxonomies and
Sonic Vocabularies
of Everyday Sounds

Vanderveer
*Acoustical, Action, Excitation or
Source Similarity*

Guastavino
*Acoustical, Location or Activity
Similarity*

Guyot
*Acoustical, Action, Excitation or
Source Similarity*

Lemaitre et al.
*Acoustic, Action, Excitation or
Source Similarity*

i) Acoustic Similarity
ii) Causal Similarity
iii) Semantic Similarity

Marcell et al.
*Action, Excitation, Location or
Activity Similarity*

Brazil et al.
*Action, Source, Activity or
Location Similarity*

Gerard
*Action, Excitation, Location or
Activity Similarity*

Gaver
*Acoustical, Action, Excitation or
Source Similarity*

Mullins et al.
*Action, Excitation, Location or
Activity Similarity*

Fig. 10.5 A summary and key features of existing sound-perception taxonomies

Chapter 11
Emotions

Abstract The emotional dimension of sonic interaction is expressed through subtle variations within a single sound object and across articulations of sound events, with possible interaction with the other senses.

11.1 Emotions in sonic gestures

Simple, everyday actions such as knocking on a door can indeed communicate emotions. A deep understanding of this fact may lead to effective technological augmentations of everyday objects.

The specific phenomenon of door knocking has been thoroughly investigated by Renzo Vitale in an experiment performed at KTH [143]. Subjects were asked to knock on a door with different emotional intentions, and their performances were recorded with high-end acoustic equipment and with a visual motion capture system. Some descriptors such as inter-onset interval, average rms sound power, and number of knocks were extracted. An emotion-recognition test was run with other subjects, with the audio recordings of knocking sounds as stimuli. It was shown that some emotions (e.g., afraid, angry) are much better detected than others (e.g., tired, excited). It was shown that the available descriptors do not allow to extract some of the emotions unambiguously, thus explaining the poor performance of subjects with the recognition of these emotions.

11.2 Rhetorics in sonic interaction

Although rhetoric is commonly defined as the art or technique of persuasion through the use of oral or written language, its scope can be extended to other fields. Since the sixteenth century several theoreticians explained how instrumental music can be effectively organized and structured in time in order to achieve a more understandable form. In this respect, rhetoric addresses both the logical and emotional spheres of the listener. Pietro Polotti has been extending the principles of rhetoric to functional product sounds and to audio communication [106]. In a Short-Term Scientific Mission at IRCAM-Paris he collaborated with Guillaume Lemaitre at designing and testing earcons for an hypothetical operating system. They prepared rhetoric and non-rhetoric earcons for actions such as copy, paste, undo, etc.. They measured a number of correct associations (earcon with action) that increases with the number of trials. For some actions, the adoption of a rhetoric scheme led to a number of correct associations that is statistically larger than what could be achieved with non-rhetoric earcons [107].

11.3 Audio-visual computer animation

Producing an animation film is always a time-consuming process that does not end when the characters are animated. Sound design usually comes after finishing the animation process, to add music, speech, and sound effects. Ideally the link between image and sound should start right from the beginning of the production process, as the perceived mood of a character results from a combination of its visual and auditory appearance. Many years of experience in analysis-by-synthesis, and the production of sophisticated tools such as `Director Musices`, have made KTH, Stockholm one of the leading centers for research in music emotions. João Cordeiro visited KTH to develop an extension of `Director Musices` aimed at the production of audio-visual animations. His tool `pDaniM` (see figure 11.1) is dedicated to directors, producers, sound designers, and animators, and it can be seen as a sonic parallel of animatics, a technique used in animation to feel the sense of time in the movie [18].

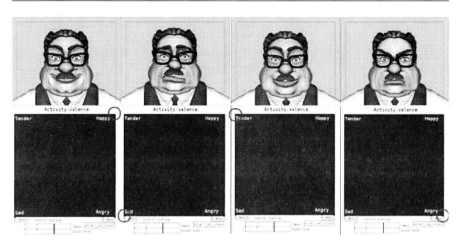

Fig. 11.1 The mood of a character on the Activity-Valence plane

Chapter 12
Spatial sonic interaction

Abstract The coupling between sound and space does not only mean projection, spatialization, or surround anymore. The physical space affords sound-mediated exploration, narration, social interaction and performance.

12.1 Audio augmented environments

Martin Rumori, in his Short-Term Scientific Mission at the University of Music and Dramatic Arts in Graz, exploited the CUBE space, a medium sized concert hall equipped with a 24-channel loudspeaker system and with a Vicon optical tracking system. He implemented a headphone-based sound spatialization system for exploration of sounds in space. For dynamic soundscape exploration with headphones there is the problem of interpolating time-varying Head-Related Transfer Functions (HRTF). In order to overcome this problem Rumori proposed a spatialization system based on virtual Ambisonics, which simulates the 24 loudspeakers and uses HRTFs for signals going from the virtual (fixed) loudspeakers to the listener's ears. The room effect is included in the measured HRTFs. One interesting application is illustrated in figure 12.1, where two tracking targets are clearly visible in the user's head and hand. The first is used to keep track of position and orientation of the listener in both the physical and the virtual space, and the second is used to explore the space where the virtual sound sources are located.

The CUBE system in Graz has been further exploited in the COST Action on Sonic Interaction Design, especially by its working group on Interactive Art and

Fig. 12.1 Exploring a virtual soundscape while moving in a physical space.

Music. The Tracked Hand-held Speaker (THS) is a CUBE-based setup proposed by Gerhard Eckel for collective experimentation. The THS is a small speaker which can easily be held in one hand. The tracking markers allow the speaker to be tracked in 6 degrees of freedom with high spatial (about 1 mm) and temporal resolution (120 Hz)[1]. Since the speaker is held in the hand, lower frequencies are also sensed haptically.

12.2 Unfolding sonic narratives in space

The CUBE audio augmented environment in Graz was used by Johanna Gampe to explore possible transformations of the structure of linear narration into non-linear interaction through embodied experiences. Her realization adds to contributions of SID to the practices of dramatic arts (see also section 3). The active "spectator" can actually enter the space of each single character and experience a narrative path that unfolds in time as well as in space according to her movements on stage. Moreover, the so-called back sphere can be introduced as theatrical dimension that can be aesthetically challenged with new dramaturgical ideas. A first attempt in understanding the socio-psychology of sonic space in a theatrical context was done through questionnaires [42].

---

[1] Video demonstration: http://vimeo.com/5379935

12.3 Playing with sound in space

Exploration and exploitation of the auditory space for artistic purposes is also one of the central themes of Daniël Ploeger installations [104]. In a STSM to Aalto University he studied different strategies to simulate loudspeaker movement in the medial plane. In another Mission to the Bauhaus University in Weimar he explored the body space and developed a performance suit equipped with biometric sensors and a loudspeaker. In his performances with the suit, Ploeger proposed a sort of dialogue between the visceral body and technological devices (see figure 12.2). Evaluation was performed based on reactions of the public and the realization was accordingly refined [103]. In a theoretical framework, it was argued that the technological representations of the body in a feedback loop may be read as a constellation of multiple, fragmented doubles [105].

Fig. 12.2 Daniël Ploeger performing with the sounding suit

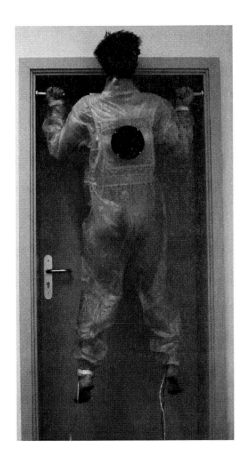

12.4 Interactive sound installations

Jan Schacher has been working at interactive audio-visual installations aimed at engaging an audience in exploratory behaviors. His STSM at at McGill University was a fact-finding mission concerning machine learning, spatial audio, and strategies to map gestures to audio-visual behaviors [123]. His findings have been applied to an audio-visual interactive installation (Codespace, figure 12.3) which has seen a number of different incarnations and deals with audience engagement in different ways. Codespace was commissioned for the Today's Art festival at the Hague in the Netherlands in 2005. After the STSM, a new edition was shown at the Media Art Lab of the Art Museum in Graz, Austria in early 2009.

Interacting with an instrument or a reactive installation always entails a process of learning, exploring and adapting. The experience in interaction with technical systems enables us to adapt to new situations by projecting and optimizing tentative gestures based on the feedback the system provides. The interaction mode of Codespace was based on a multi-touch surface. The visitor is exposed to spatial ambisonic audio [124], and to some large video projections showing flocking motion. Through human-flock interaction, the mappings adapt and learn about audience behavior, thus reinforcing audience engagement in particular during the initial moments of an encounter.

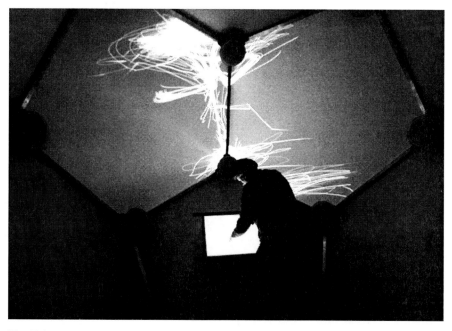

Fig. 12.3 Adaptive mapping installation at Walcheturm Gallery in Zurich, January 2009

Chapter 13
Sketching and prototyping

Abstract Lo-fi and hi-fi prototyping require different means and strategies. In the early stage of the design process, sketches of sonic interactions can be achieved through clever use of audio-visual materials and techniques. The narrative dimension of sonic interactions, even when they are mimicked with very simple means, allows designers to grow new ideas and avoid pitfalls.

13.1 On the appropriateness of sound

Sandra Pauletto of the Department of Theatre, Film and Television of York University conducted a research aimed at transferring some knowledge from the world of sound effects for films to Sonic Interaction Design at large. In her Short-Term Scientific Mission to KTH, Stockholm, Pauletto considered a film excerpt of human-object interaction (see figure 13.1), decomposed it in a set of discernible sound objects, and prepared a set of different alternative sound effects by amplitude and frequency manipulations of the original sounds. Then, a pool of subjects were asked to rate the proposed sounds for appropriateness and similarity to the original. It turned out that the higher the similarity with the original sound, the more appropriate the sound was found for the action represented. This result encourages further studies on the practices of film sound design, so that part of the existing expertise can be applied to SID. This kind of cross-fertilization was also experienced at the workshop on theatrical methods held in York (see Chapter 3).

Fig. 13.1 Two frames from the excerpt of Terminator 2 used in the Pauletto's experiment

13.2 A video platform for alternative sound designs

A bibliography of sounding products, a so-called productography[1], was collected by the COST Action on Sonic Interaction Design. Some Action's members created a framework for categorizing these products within ten categories. Products were then collected through email requests, and entered to the Productography via an online form, in which contributors specified the product attributes in the different categories. The presentation format consists of a textual description of the product, according to the different attributes, and links to additional information.

Starting from the observation that video is widely used both after and before the implementation of interactive products, Michal Rinott conceived a web platform for experimenting with different sonic overlays of a given filmed interaction. With such a tool, different design approaches and sonic materials could be explored and exemplified, such as vocal sketching (see Chapter 4), or the use of inspirations and excerpts extracted from movie sound. Such exploration could be organized as a social activity, for example by organizing sound design challenges around a specific interaction, as illustrated in figure 13.2.

13.3 Audio films

A collaboration between York University and the Portuguese Chatolic University allowed Mariana Julieta López to experiment with new forms of cinematic communication for visually impaired persons. In particular, in her STSM, López realized a scene of an audio film, i.e. a sound-based work where all the information necessary

---

[1] http://www.cost-sid.org/wiki/WG2Product/Examples

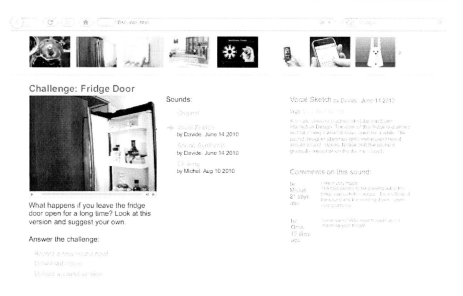

Fig. 13.2 A look and feel prototype for a web-based sound design challenge

to understand the story, including actions, spaces, movement and interaction, are provided through sound. The difference with radio drama is that an audio film does not use any spoken commentary. The proposed audio film was later completed and the effectiveness of rendering characters and environments was tested with a pool of listeners. Among other things, the effectiveness of sound effects, soundmarks, dialogues, footsteps, and reverb in characterizing different spaces was assessed [74], and this study received the best-paper award at the International Conference on Auditory Display in Copenhagen in 2009. The results, together with sound excerpts, can be found in an online[2] journal publication [75]. The possibility of minimizing or eliminating speech in audio films was further explored by López and Pauletto at York University [76], and they found how in many cases a spoken voice overrides concurrent sound cues. This research has also relevance for sound in games (see section 15.5) and for audio-only games.

13.4 Vocal sketching

Several STSMs stemmed from the workshop on sketching in Sonic Interaction Design described in chapter 4. On a longer time scale, they allowed to experiment on the possibility of using the voice as a sketching tool and on the narrative aspects of sketching SID.

---

[2] http://www.musicandmeaning.net/issues/showArticle.php?artID=8.2

In his research, Loïc Kessous has been interested in the emotional content of gesture and voice, trying to extract and exploit them in multimodal interactions [16, 60]. In the STSM at the Holon Institute of Technology, Kessous experimented with the voice as a tool that sound designers may use to carve recorded or synthetic sounds. In order to do that, a gap should be bridged, between the tools that are available for audio recording (see figure 13.3) and analysis, and the professional software that are used for sound editing. A first attempt at filling this gap has been made through the encoding of the extracted salient vocal features into MIDI control messages, that are later used in the audio editor.

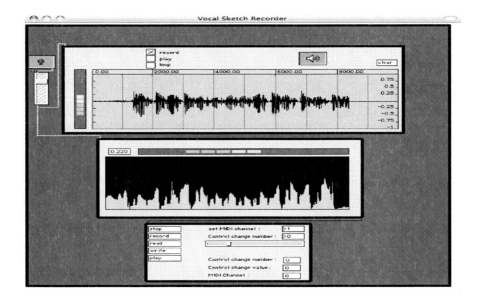

Fig. 13.3 The Vocal Sketch Recorder as a Max/MSP patch

The goal of the Voice-Gesture Sketching Tool (VOGST) project, started by Karmen Franinovic in a STSM in Holon, is to develop a tool for sketching and improvising sonic interaction through voice and gesture. The relations between sound, artifact and gesture are seen as the core materials of sonic interaction design, and the major efforts are directed towards sketching the coupling between bodily movement and sonic feedback. The first version of the VOGST is a simple abstract object with embedded sensing and sound technology (see figure 13.4) which has the capability of recording the voice and simultaneously capturing the gesture performed. The multiple sounds recorded can be replayed and manipulated by re-enacting the associated gestures with the VOGST. The system uses Gesture Follower (in Max/MSP) developed by Frédéric Bevilacqua and Bruno Zamborlin [8]. The results of evaluation with designers showed the benefits of a quick and direct way of capturing gesture-sounds for the communication and exploration of interaction concepts. Many participants enjoyed the possibilities of transforming the recorded

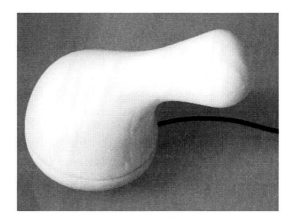

Fig. 13.4 The gesture/voice capture device VOGST

sounds by changing the qualities of gestures (e.g., speed, repetition) confirming that gestural sound is inherently expressive. Overall, the VOGST proved to well suit the sketching of creatively and physically engaging sound applications and products.

13.5 Telling stories with sound

Tal Drori and Enrico Costanza used their STSM at the Holon Institute of Technology to explore the ways in which children use their voices to augment story-telling with sounds. They designed and implemented a low-cost prototype tangible user interface that enables children to record and manipulate sounds in a playful way. The system is based on a mobile phone and a set of cards with visual markers on them (see figure 13.5): these are visual symbols that work both as figurative icons as well as markers recognizable by a mobile phone running a special recognition application. This joint STSM, and the contiguous workshop, facilitated the fusion and evolution of two prior projects: "Audio d-touch" by Costanza [20] and "Pixel Materiali" by Drori and Rinott [28]. From a technical point of view, the system is based on the older projects, which made it possible to create a functional prototype in very short time. When given to children, the figurative markers were naturally combined with utterances of various kinds to create stories. Much of the engagement came from the gradual construction of narrative soundscapes by vocal production, recording, and playback.

13.6 Articulating the aesthetics of sound in interaction

The STSM of Stefano Delle Monache at Aalto University was aimed at developing and testing the design processes that would have been used in the TS on Product Sound Design (chapter 8). This was done through exploratory activities at the De-

Fig. 13.5 A story made out of visual markers

sign Factory of Aalto University. In particular, Stefano Delle Monache, Daniel Hug and Cumhur Erkut collaborated at an interpretive process of co-design that aims at transferring a narrative sound design strategy, as found in movies, to the sonic aesthetics of physical manipulations [23]. The abstract qualities described in the narration include energy, use, and control. For example, in a squeezing action a friction sound may guide balancing, a rolling sound may affect perceived effort, and another sound may reflect energy dissipation (see figure 13.6). The interpretive approach retains the holistic quality of the interactive experience, while allowing the examination of its expressional, interactional and technical aspects.

Fig. 13.6 Physical sketching of an abstract design concept

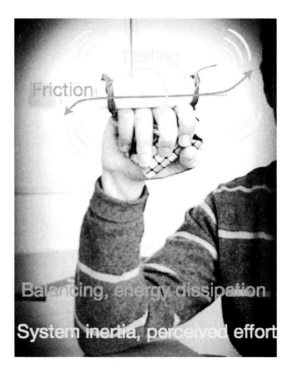

The underlying idea of Daniel Hug's research is to work out narrative and performative strategies for sound design in SID. In this respect, the domains of film and game provide a wealth of "good cases" of narrative sound to study. In the last few years, Hug organized and was involved in many workshops, in a participatory research process which allowed to explore narrativity in product sound design [56]. His STSM at IRCAM-Paris focused on two aspects: a) understanding the requirements and methods of sound design practicians involved in industry-oriented projects and b) investigating methods of sound generation for their aesthetic and pragmatic potential. Hug's heuristic framework, based on situational criteria and narrative metatopics, bridges the gap between design, branding, sound design, and musical concepts, thus supporting the crossfertilization of these disciplines. The STSM, thanks to interviews and hands-on sessions with expert designers, set the foundation for the development of a prototypical design process, including evaluation methods, that can be used in a commercial context.

Chapter 14
Protocols, tools, and curricula

Abstract Interoperability is a great concern for the designer of interactive systems. Several important contributions have been made to establish standards and protocols, as well as to support them in tools and applications. A widespread and effective use of such tools can be boosted through pedagogical programs and activities.

14.1 Including gestures into interchange formats

Since the introduction of MIDI in 1992 the industry and research on music technology has been opening new ways to connect a variety of devices to form ecologies of digital processors, sensors, and actuators. A more modern protocol based on UDP/IP networking is Open Sound Control (OSC), also developed in the computer music community and being used in the wider context of interactive arts. A similar trend is observed in the development and diffusion of other formats whose definition is driven by the needs of computer musicians. The Sound Description Interchange Format (SDIF[1]) is focused on well-defined and extensible interchange of sound descriptions including spectral, sinusoidal, or time-domain sound models. SDIF consists of a basic data format framework and an extensible set of standard sound descriptions.

The COST Action on Sonic Interaction Design, having prominent interest in human gestures as causes of sounds in interaction, has contributed to the develop-

---

[1] `http://sdif.sourceforge.net/`

ment of the Gesture Description Interchange Format (GDIF[2]), aiming at storing and streaming descriptions of gesture qualities, performer-instrument relationships, and movement-sound relationships in a coherent and consistent way. The main platform for testing GDIF is Max/MSP and its Jamoma framework[3], being maintained at BEK in Norway.

In his Short-Term Scientific Mission, Kristian Nymoen investigated the use of SDIF as a container format for GDIF recordings. Recording GDIF data to SDIF files may solve many problems related to synchronization of data from different sources. Using the facilities of McGill University, including Vicon-460 motion capture, Polhemus 6DOF position sensing, and Phantom Omni haptic sensing, it was possible to make challenging experiments with bidirectional data streams. Nymoen developed some Jamoma modules that have been made available to the sound and music computing community. Advantages of using the methods presented here include the possibility to record any kind of numerical data from several sources independent of sample rate. These tools were used by Nymoen for his own research on co-articulation in piano performance [43, 58].

In another STSM at KTH, Alexander Refsum Jensenius improved the Max/MSP-based tools for recording, playing back, and analyzing data. He developed several new Jamoma models that have been made available to the gesture research community. The SID recorder, for example, is shown on figure 14.1. This research line and the development of its related tools were boosted, before the SID COST Action, by the COST Action on Gesture Controlled Audio Systems (ConGAS), finished in 2007. More recently, a book collected the most relevant scientific results of the ConGAS Action [44], including significant contributions to research on Sonic Interaction Design [59].

14.2 Audio environments for mobile devices

Mobile devices and embedded systems are often challenged by sophisticated sound synthesis and processing methods, as their computational resources and screen real estate are limited. Specific efforts have been made to redirect popular sound software environments towards these specific architectures. One popular platform for sound designers [36] is Pure Data (pd). Tim Redfern took the opportunity of a Short-Term Scientific Mission at the University Pompeu Fabra in Barcelona to work with Gunter Geiger at improving a port of pd for the Gumstix Linux platform. He also contributed flite~, an open-source speech synthesizer, to such pd port, thus providing more sonification capabilities to embedded systems.

---

[2] http://www.gdif.org/
[3] http://www.jamoma.org/

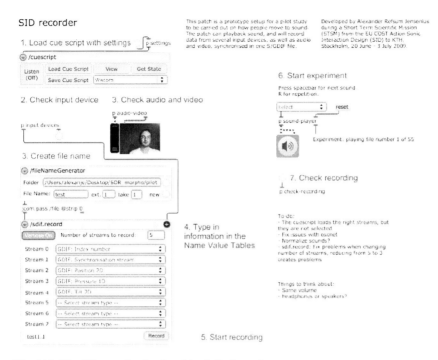

Fig. 14.1 The SID recorder developed by A. R. Jensenius

14.3 Instruments for a sonic pedagogy

Richard Widerberg has been working, for some years, at a broad platform called IM-PROVe, for working pedagogically and creatively with sound. The platform includes workshops, often held in schools, where field recordings provide the materials that are later discussed and used in a music improvisation. Since the IMPROVe project is a broad platform for working pedagogically and creatively with sound, Widerberg dedicated a STSM in Porto to interact with the people behind the Digitòpia project of Casa da Musica (see chapter 7). In that mission, the software platform was extended to include a new control layer for sound object manipulation, based on commonly available gamepads (see figure 14.2). On December 10th 2010 the improved IMPROVe sound object instrument was used and tested at a music festival for young people at Mölnlycke Kulturhus in Sweden.

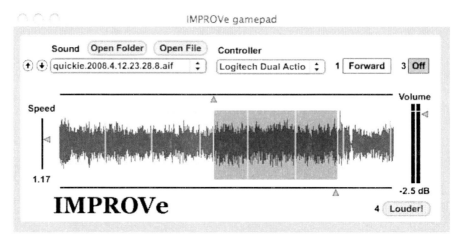

Fig. 14.2 The IMPROVe sound object instrument for gamepad

14.4 An interdisciplinary curriculum on Sonic Interaction Design

A discipline that is emerging from research, such as Sonic Interaction Design, has to face the problem of transferring methods, practices, and knowledge to students. There are several academic sites that, in the last few years, have established curricula or classes on SID: Prominent examples are found at Zurich University of the Arts, at Aalto University in Helsinki, at Aalborg University Copenhagen (Medialogy), at York University, at the Portuguese Catholic University, at IUAV University of Venice, at KTH Stockholm, and at the Holon Institute of Technology. All of these institutions have been involved in several activities of the COST Action on SID (see also chapters 3, 4, and 8).

Rolf Nordahl of Medialogy dedicated his STSM in Italy to discuss a prospect of SID education with colleague educators at the IUAV University of Venice and at the HCIed Conference held in Rome [89]. A set of key competences for sonic interaction designers was outlined, and the experiences of problem-based learning [90, 61] were publicly illustrated and discussed. The discussions produced the following categories of key competences:

1. auditory perception;
2. auditory communication;
3. audio-visual interaction;
4. sound synthesis and processing;
5. aesthetical and emotional issues;
6. design exercises;
7. evaluation of sonic interaction design.

Particularly critical is the problem of targeting education on sound synthesis and processing to students whose main interest is in designing interactive products rather than developing new sound computing methods. The tools designed for audio engineers and researchers are difficult to master for design students and the need for special front ends and ready-made patches has emerged (see also chapter 8). Another issue is that of evaluation, where quantitative and psychophysical methods are seldom practical to evaluate design artifacts. More work on selecting and communicating useful and practical design-based evaluation methods needs to be done [91].

Chapter 15
Sonification

Abstract Relevant information are often multidimensional and varying dynamically with human actions. The capability of sound to afford pattern discovery even in conditions of shared or peripheral attention makes information sonification very relevant in a variety of fields such as biology, sport, or games.

15.1 Sonification of 3D dynamics

Dynamical 3D data are the raw material in many contemporary research fields. Florian Grond has been developing a framework that handles these data types and allows rapid prototyping of information sonification. In a Short-Term Scientific Mission at McGill University, Florian Grond focused on two classes of data: One derived from motion-capture systems applied to music instrumentalists, and the other coming from macro molecular dynamics [47]. By tight interaction with Thomas Hermann (see section 10.3), Grond developed a data pre-processor in `Python`, based on principal-component analysis, and classes for real-time sonification in `SuperCollider`. Research on sonification of ancillary gestures of musicians was further developed as a joint work between Bielefeld and McGill universities [48]. Research on sonification of molecular structures was also further developed and presented at the Interactive Sonification Workshop [49] (see chapter 5).

Fig. 15.1 Clusters of urban activities

15.2 Urban signals

Stephan Baumann's research project Urban Sync collected and examined urban signals, looking for correlates of personal well-being. He conducted three weeks of STSM in the city of Porto and collected urban and personal signals over extensive periods of time. Equipped with an audio recorder, a GPS datalogger, an "electronic-smog" scanner, and a wristband for detecting heart rate, skin conductance, and acceleration, Baumann collected a variety of signals that a person is immersed in over the course of an hour, a day, a week. A total of forty-five hours of signals have been recorded and shared with other researchers, as an Open-Reality Data stream. A first challenge is how to make sense of this stream, through meaningful visualizations or sonifications. In particular, making the GHz signals audible offers great potential when thinking about the design of context-aware displays. A second range of applications may derive from data mining, for example by combining GPS and accelerometer data to achieve a sort of retrieval by movement. This possibility was investigated in the TS held in Porto in 2009 (see chapter 7).

Figure 15.1 shows a `GoogleEarth` view of some clusters of urban activities, representing segments and paths that are extracted through k-means clustering on audio represented as Mel-Frequency Cepstral Coefficients.

15.3 Sports

As demonstrated in the workshop described in chapter 5, sports are interesting application frameworks for research in sonification. Nina Schaffert of the University of Hamburg established a collaboration with Stephen Barrass of the University of Canberra, and a set of experiments were performed over Europe and Australia on amateur and elite athletes. This was made possible by an agreement between the Australian Academy of Science and COST[1]. The key question of this research thread is: How is it possible to transfer the sound information into meaningful information for the movement process? The purpose may be that of increasing the effectiveness of training for elite athletes, but the evaluation of a sonification scheme is not easily reduced to a collection of measurements. The aesthetics of a sonification play an important role, especially when training have to be sustained over time [126]. The work presented by Schaffert at the International Conference on Auditory Display in 2009 [127], awarded with the best-poster prize, gave conceptual considerations for a sound design to fulfill the specific purpose of movement optimization that would be acceptable to elite athletes. In this respect, a sonification probe that can be rapidly customized to the taste of the individual athlete proved to be very effective [6]. It is interesting to notice how some countries are investing in research programs for sonification in sport science[2].

15.4 Physiology

Another activity made possible by the agreement between the Australian Academy of Science and COST (see also section 15.3) was the STSM performed at Starlab Barcelona by Stephen Barrass of the University of Canberra. The purpose of the STSM was to prototype and develop realtime sonifications for the Enobio portable wireless EEG device that is being commercialized by Starlab. The sonifications supplement visual and statistical analysis by allowing users to listen to temporal information in EEG data from the Enobio. The EEG signals are mapped into sound in real-time with specially designed sonification algorithms. This mapping was used in a violin-cello-EEG trio concert at the University of Pompeu Fabra in Barcelona on the evening of 22 July, during the Sound and Music Computing (SMC) Conference in 2010 (see figure 15.2).

15.5 Games

Gaming is one of the most active application fields of Sonic Interaction Design, a field where interactive generation of high-quality sounds and images is the principal research focus. In his STSM at Bielefeld University, Louise Valgerður Nickerson investigated the sonification of grid-based games. Grid-based games provide a controlled and well-defined test bed for the sonification of grid-organised data. The main characteristic of grids that makes them interesting to study is that it is important to have an idea of context. Each data point on its own is relatively meaningless, while a set of data points can together represent a pattern of interest. In music,

[1] http://www.science.org.au/internat/europe/cost.html
[2] Project IIA1-070802/09 – German Federal Institute of Sport Science; SONEA Project – Swedish Olympic Performance Centre

Fig. 15.2 Sasha Agranov (cello) rehearsing for SMC Conference concert

one axis of a grid is often associated with time, and the resulting pattern of sound events (the other axis may be pitch) is often looped. Grids are also the supporting structure of cellular automata, where local disturbances propagate through neighborhoods. These two metaphors, the music loop and the cellular automaton were used by Nickerson to sonify two games: Connect Four and Sudoku. The games were implemented and an extensive evaluation was performed on Connect Four [86].

Chapter 16
Virtual and mixed realities

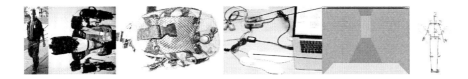

Abstract Diving into virtual environments, having robots as avatars, or just augmenting everyday experiences are all activities that challenge the designers of sound-based interaction loops. As far as sonic-interaction embodiments are concerned, advances in knowledge and understanding are being produced by artists, scientists, and engineers.

16.1 Tele-presence

Creating an instantaneous and effective perception-action loop that spans real and virtual worlds is an ambitious research goal, not only for scientists, but also for some artists. One of the most prominent of such artists is Suguru Goto, who opened the 2009 Music Biennale in Venice with a robotic drumming performance[1]. In his STSM to the Kunsthochschule für Medien in Cologne, Germany, he made an important step toward realizing a two-way relation between augmented body and virtual body. In Goto's project, an avatar in a virtual environment (e.g., `Second Life`) is controlled by movements of the (augmented) human body, and the human body may be affected by movements of an avatar, by means of an actuated exoskeleton called Powered Suit [45, 46]. A performative multimedia piece by Goto based on

---

[1] `http://www.youtube.com/watch?v=z1faj2WqQRc`

Fig. 16.1 Powered Suit and BodySuit

the sensing suit (called BodySuit) is *L'homme transcendé*[2], and the bidirectional control link has been exploited in the performance *netBody*[3].

16.2 Dancing robots

Many scientists think that the relation between intelligence and the morphology of the body may rely in a dynamic interaction between body, brain and environment. In this context, dance is seen as a collection of expressive gestural behaviours that emerge from a body's morphology, shaped by the corporeal responses to musical stimuli and cultural involvement.

In his STSM at Ghent University, João Lobato Oliveira was interested in methods for mapping human dance motion primitives (keyposes), previously extracted with a 3D motion capture system, onto humanoid robots, while preserving the musical entrainment and the naturalness of performance. Oliveira's research benefited from a collaboration with Luiz Naveda, who has been studying the gestures of samba dance (see chapter 18). The results of this collaboration were presented at the Workshop on Robots and Musical Expressions in Taipei [94], a presentation that was awarded with a COST-ICT ESR Conference Grant. To model the reciprocal and dynamical coupling between body and brain, perception and action, a real-time audio beat-tracker [93] supports on-line feedback control through which the robot may adjust the perceptual rhythmic metrical level to its morphological naturalness (see figure 16.2.

---

[2] http://www.youtube.com/watch?v=KVkv_7X-5mY
[3] http://0141712186.free.fr/Contents2/netBody/netBody-e.html

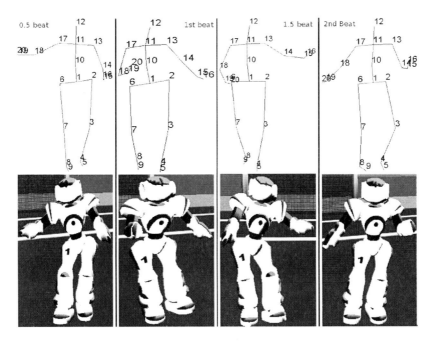

Fig. 16.2 Mapping human samba dancing patterns onto a humanoid robot model, with half-beat granularity

16.3 Sonic interactive walking

The COST Action SID had intense scientific exchanges with a 7FP EU Project called NIW[4] (Natural Interactive Walking - ICT-2007.8.0 FET Open). The NIW project aims at the design and evaluation of floor interfaces, to exploit the synergy of perception and action in capturing and guiding human walking, by means of audio-haptic shoes or tiles. Indeed, the SID Action could be accounted among the starters of the NIW project, as the early research activities were initiated in SID in the year 2008, before NIW was officially approved and started. One of these activities was a STSM of Stefania Serafin (Aalborg University Copenhagen) at the University of Verona, where she prototyped two sound synthesis algorithms and one control algorithm for the real-time audio rendering of footsteps. Evolutions of these early software prototypes were eventually used for sensed and actuated shoes and used in a variety of behavioral studies [92, 88, 138, 139, 142]. The sensing part of the system used in Copenhagen by Serafin and colleagues was enhanced by Birgit Gasteiger in another STSM. She built a setup using force-sensing resistors, accelerometers, and gyroscopes, as illustrated in figure 16.3.

A NIW-related experiment was run by Luca Turchet in his STSM at INRIA, Rennes. The hosting laboratory is well known for visual pseudo-haptics, i.e. the

---

[4] http://www.niwproject.eu/

Fig. 16.3 The sensed shoes, as prepared by Birgit Gasteiger

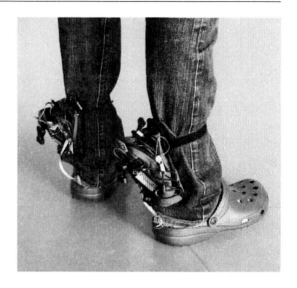

rendering of haptic effects by manipulation of visual motion, through multisensory illusions. One of these effects is the visual simulation of bumps and holes, that in some conditions is perceived as a haptic, force-feedback effect, even when the exploratory device is passive. Turchet contributed the sound synthesis of footsteps that, when included in an audio-visual virtual environment, allowed to test the effectiveness of bump and hole rendering under the different modalities. Moreover, it was possible to assess which of the visual or the auditory modalities dominates in presence of conflicting cues [137].

In Turchet's experiments the control of the pace of footsteps was the key to convey an auditory rendering of bumps and holes. The real-time detection of the walking pace was the goal of the STSM of Bart Moens at McGill University. This can be considered as a preliminary building block, not only for virtual environments such as those investigated by Turchet, but also for the design of many interactive objects, for a wide spectrum of applications ranging from rehabilitation to entertainment. Moens studied and compared, with quantitative and qualitative methods, different detection algorithms based on accelerometers, gyroscopes, and force-sensing resistors. The qualitative evaluation was done using sonification (see also chapter 15) of the heel-strikes, thus providing subjective feedback about the quality of the algorithm in terms of accuracy and delay. The sensing system used the same Xsens technology used in the Interactive Dance Project (figure 16.4; see also section 18.3 in chapter 18). Moens analyzed five locations on the human body: left and right ankle, left pocket, left upper arm, and hip. Using a force-sensing sensor as a ground truth, he could find optimal combinations of sensor position and signal-processing algorithms for both step frequency and heel strike detection [83].

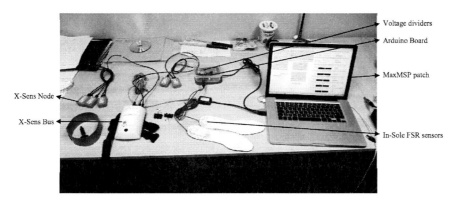

Fig. 16.4 The data logging setup for step frequency and heel strike detection

Chapter 17
Tangible interfaces

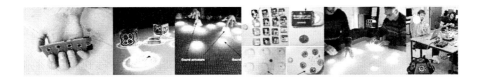

Abstract The last decade has seen a flourishing of new musical instruments, based on the new possibilities offered by sensors, actuators, and communication technologies. Among these, a few tabletop surfaces emerged as successful devices both for artistic and scientific research. Beyond short-term fascination, the development of a virtuosity in the long term is possible only if special attention is given to the design for our sensitive fingers.

17.1 Tables

The Reactable is a musical instrument in the form of an interactive table. It was born at the Pompeu Fabra University in Barcelona in 2003, taken on tour by Björk in 2007, and put on the market in 2010 in three versions: for stage performance, for group interaction in public spaces, and for mobile devices[1]. Kjetil Falkenberg Hansen and Smilen Dimitrov entered this success story of sound and music computing in 2008, with two coordinated STSMs in Barcelona. Indeed, one of the Reactable developers, Marcos Alonso, started a collaboration with Falkenberg Hansen already in 2006, as part of the COST Action on Gesture Controlled Audio Systems (ConGAS) [44]. Falkenberg Hansen is a musicologist who studied and modeled the techniques used by professional DJ scratchers [34]. His objective for the STSM was to continue the integration of scratch models into the reactable and

---

[1] http://www.reactable.com

Fig. 17.1 The `Reactable`
objects for DJ scratching

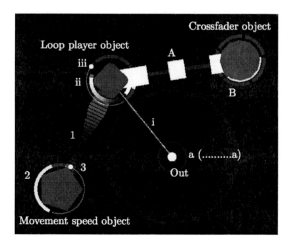

to study the interaction by using a DJ and a `Reactable` player as test subjects. The evaluation led to the development of new objects, graphically represented in figure 17.1, for the `Reactable` library [32, 35].

Dimitrov, on the other hand, was interested in implementing new `Reactable` objects for controlling sound models of friction [25], and possibly in combining them with DJ scratching [33]. Sliding an object on a smooth surface may easily produce squeals or other friction sounds, so it is quite natural to think of sliding tracked objects to control synthetic friction sounds. Less obvious and more interesting is the combination of two tracked objects to mimic the action on a source-bow couple of objects, as in violin playing (see figure 17.2).

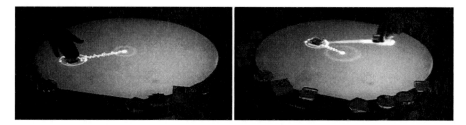

Fig. 17.2 A friction object (left) and a source-bow couple (right) on the `Reactable`

Another tabletop surface that is attracting the attention of some researchers of the SMC community is `Tangisense`, developed at Multicom-LIG in Grenoble [1]. The interactive table is based on an array of RFID antennas for object tracking and on a LED matrix for visual feedback and for virtual-object representation (see figure 17.3). Jean-Julien Filatriau visited Multicom-LIG to perform a sonic-texture grouping experiment based on the `Tangisense`, with the goal of drawing a collective map of sonic textures based on multidimensional scaling of participants responses [37]. Eventually, such map may be used to guide navigation in the space of

sonic textures. Navigation can be performative, as Filatriau demonstrated by organizing sound textures as attractors in space and by dynamically exploring the surface
with actuator objects[2].

Fig. 17.3 A subject performing a sonic-texture grouping
task with the `Tangisense`

17.2 Devices for the hand and fingers

In the history of SMC there are many examples of innovative musical instruments,
but only a few players of computer-based musical instruments actually developed
some form of virtuosity. One of these is Michel Waisvisz, who invented, refined,
and mastered `The Hands`, an expressive musical performance interface developed
in the nineteen-eighties. Dan Overholt, in a STSM at the University of Oslo, took
inspiration from `The Hands` and started the development of `The Fingers`, a
controller made of two parts, for coordinated use of the two hands. The left-hand
part is just a `Wiimote` controller with a convex mirror add-on (see figure 17.4, left)
that serves the purpose of exploiting the built-in infrared camera to detect the relative
position of the right hand. The right part is a set of small sensorpads, each being
a sort of flat 3D joystick (see figure 17.4, right). Additional sensing capabilities
and the connection between the two parts is provided by a microcontroller-based
board. Overholt has an extensive experience in developing new musical instruments,
from which he derived a theoretical framework based on human-centered design
approaches [96].

---

[2] `http://www.tele.ucl.ac.be/~jjfil/SMC10.html`

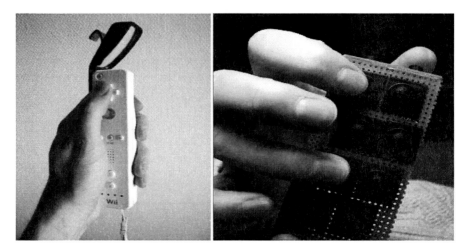

Fig. 17.4 The left and right components of The Fingers

Chapter 18
Human gestures

Abstract Gestures are at the origin of sound production, and are often also a direct consequence of sounds. Sound and music, in a sense, encode and embed gestures, in a way that is made visible through instrumental music performance and dance.

18.1 Sound from gestures, gestures from sound

Norbert Schnell of IRCAM, Paris and Gerhard Eckel of the University of Music and Dramatic Arts in Graz, Austria had an extensive collaboration on gesture sonification and gestured controlled synthesis. They explored the possibility of automatically deriving mappings between gesture and sound from recordings of movements performed by subjects while listening to a recorded sound. The experimental setting was similar to the one used for spatial exploration of sound and illustrated in figure 12.1.

18.2 Instrumental gestures

For some years, Esteban Maestre has been studying the highly-specialized gestures in bowed-string instrument performance [78]. His STSM at the University of Genova was aimed at making practical experience with the EyesWeb software platform, with the goal of enriching the application possibilities of bowed-string instrumental gesture capture into real performance scenarios. He also collaborated with Alexander R. Jensenius and Antonio Camurri toward the definition of a storage structure for gesture and sound data, as an extension of GDIF (see Chapter 14). Some of their conclusions were derived from intense discussion with the string players of the famous *Quartetto di Cremona*. Further studies in this direction have been carried on in the EU-ICT Project SAME[1].

Antonio Camurri at the University of Genova hosted the STSM of Stella Paschalidou, who is pursuing a PhD on gesticulation as an expressive support mechanism for singing practice and training. This research line takes inspiration from classical Indian music training, which is based on a score-free teacher-student relationship, where visualization through hand gestures supports vocalization in an integral multi-modal experience. Gesticulation tries to convey some aspects of the hidden dynamics of the vocal tract and, at the same time, it supports the continuum that underlies music production in the Hindustani tradition, where the space between the notes is often more important than the discrete notes themselves.

Otso Lähdeoja's research aimed at providing a layer of real-time sound processing to music performance, based on ancillary gestures, i.e. instrumentalist's movements that do not directly inject energy into the sound production process. Players shake their head, shift their weight, and make anticipatory gestures that provide a wealth of information that can be used to control the augmented part of the instrument while not requiring full conscious control. In Lähdeoja's STSM, gesture data were mapped to signal-processing parameters through a physical model (springs and masses) in order to establish a non-direct yet natural relationship between gesture and sound [66, 67].

Also in the context of ancillary gestures, and in relation with gesture coarticulation being investigated by Tommaso Bianco (see chapter 9), Baptiste Caramiaux's STSM at McGill University developed a method to find a proper segmentation, by learning gesture segments from a given sound segmentation. The segment models go beyond variance-based methods [15] by introducing temporal modeling. They are based on primitives which correspond to temporal segments that must be compared with the signal segments. Topological constraints narrow down the segmentation process, as depicted in figure 18.1. The segmental model returns a sequence of gesture segments to describe the temporal evolution of the input signal according to a given set of segments. Experimental results with six clarinet players and six viola players showed that the accompanist gestures are consistent and that such consistency does not depend on the chosen granularity of segmentation.

18.3 Dance and music

Luiz Naveda obtained a PhD from Ghent University in 2010 after some years of analyses of dance and music performances, based on cross-modal methods that com-

---

[1] http://www.sameproject.eu/

Fig. 18.1 Model for segmentation of gestures

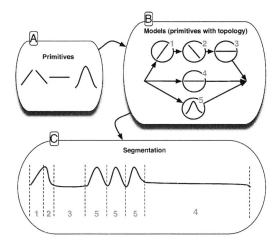

bined information from both movement and music domains. His studies had great
benefit from a collaboration with the sound and music computing research groups
based in Porto. In particular, Naveda developed a novel methodology for the analysis of micro-timing in dance and music, based on manual annotation combined with
automatic pattern analysis and machine learning. The thorough study of excerpts of
Afro-Brazilian samba music was worth the best paper award at the Brazilian Symposium on Computer Music [84, 85]. This research demonstrated that some characteristics of musical styles might be only verifiable through compu- tational approaches,
which have a potential impact on new forms of representation of rhythm and musical styles. Moreover, the link established between the research groups in Ghent and
Porto facilitated further studies in the area of robotics (see the work of Oliveira in
chapter 16).

Dance is an inherently social phenomenon, and Yago De Quay of the University
of Porto investigated the role of interactive media in multi-participatory environments such as dance halls. In his STSM at the University of Oslo, De Quay experimented with sound and body movement in three interactive events in Oslo, using
motion capture technologies [22]. His project of Interactive Dance Club spurred innovative uses of advanced sensing devices (namely, the Xsens MVN motion capture suit[2]) [130], as well as contributions to software libraries such as Jamoma (see
chapter 14). The social implications of dancing extend beyond the dance hall, and
the involvement of a larger community through the means of internet-based social
networking is now an established reality. The performance by De Quay and University of Oslo PhD student Ståle Skogstad[3], exploiting all these technological and
social innovations, was worth the best poster award at the VERDIKT conference in
Oslo in 2010 [129].

---

[2] http://www.xsens.com/
[3] http://www.youtube.com/watch?v=HaD9MJzW59s

Fig. 18.2 Yago De Quay
performing (photo by A.R.
Jensenius)

Part IV
An Exhibition on Sonic Interaction Design

Chapter 19
SID Exhibition, Oslo 2011
Frauke Behrendt and Trond Lossius, curators

Introduction

In connection with NIME 2011 (conference on New Interfaces for Musical Expression) an exhibition on Sonic Interaction Design is curated in collaboration with the EU COST IC0601 Action on Sonic Interaction Design. The exhibition features works using sonic interaction within arts, music and design as well as examples of sonification for research and artistic purposes. The exhibition takes place at the Norwegian Museum of Science, Technology and Medicine in Oslo and opens on 29th May 2011. The call for works was very successful with more than 100 submissions. Twelve works have been selected. The Exhibition is curated by Trond Lossius (BEK - Bergen Center for Electronic Arts, Norwegian SID MC member) and Frauke Behrendt (CoDE: The Cultures of the Digital Economy Institute; German SID MC member and chair of WG3), and produced by BEK. This exhibition has been generously supported by several bodies, including the Norwegian Arts Council and the SID Cost Action. The exhibition is also part of the COST 'Year of Visibility' with generous support.

The variety of works includes:

Akousmaflore (Grégory Lasserre and Anaïs met den Ancxt): A small garden composed of living musical plants, which react individually to human gestures and to gentle contact by producing a specific sound.

Auditory Augmentation at your Fingertips (René Tünnermann, Till Bovermann, and Thomas Hermann): The auditory characteristic of a computer keyboard is altered according to the weather situation outside.

aura - the stuff that forms around you (Steve Symons): A GPS-enabled backpack and headphones to experience a unique sound world, the soundscape degraded by other users' walks.

Crush-2 (Natasha Barrett): An interactive sound-art installation exploring the microscopic forces released during the process of crushing rock.

MindBox (Christian Graupner, Roberto Zappalà, Norbert Schnell, and Nils Peters): The audience operates the levers and buttons of a modified one-armed-bandit and thereby remixes the audiovisual performance of a beatboxer.

SonicChair (Thomas Hermann and Risto Kõiva): An interactive office chair giving auditory feedback that encourages users to be more dynamic on their chair.

Klanghelm / Sonic Helmet (Satoshi Morita): 3-D sound experienced through the ears and the skull.

Swinging Suitcase (Jessica Thompson): A portable object that generates and broadcasts the sound of a flock of house sparrows in response to the act of swinging.

Random Access Lattice (Gerhard Eckel): Interactive exploration of a virtual sonic sculpture constructed from speech recordings, arranged in a three-dimensional lattice structure.

Thicket (Joshue Ott and Morgan Packard): Finger drawing that creates dense sonic and visual patterns within a space of constantly evolving scrawls.

KII - Voicetopological Interface (Michael Markert): The audiences' hands form specific gestures that imitate the opening of the mouth while speaking, and these are translated into a kind of voice.

In addition to the aforementioned works selected on basis of the open call, the Norwegian musician and artist Espen Sommer Eide has been commissioned to create a new work for the exhibition. **The Movement I-X** is a multi-touch instrument in the form of an iPad app.

All these works illustrate the large field of sonic interaction design, and especially how it can be made accessible to the wider public in an exhibition.

The exhibition is accompanied by a printed catalogue, edited by the curators. The works are also presented online[1] alongside other examples of sonic interaction design.

---

[1] http://sid.bek.no/

The Movement I-X

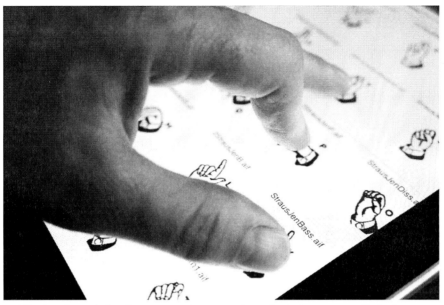

The hands and the fingers are the central manipulative organ of playing most musical instruments. A number of gestural and manipulating movements of the hand are used in playing, like fingering, picking, grasping, touching, sliding, tapping and so on.

Each of the digits has its own name and movement range. The thumb, the index finger, the middle finger, the ring finger and the little finger or the pinkie. Each finger may flex and extend, abduct and adduct, and so also circumduct. The hand has 27 bones.

It is not consciousness which touches or feels, but the hand, and the hand is, as Kant says, "an outer brain of man".

Sliders, buttons and knobs are the physical interaction interfaces of most electronic instruments. In relation to the touchscreen, the various unique aspects of the hand have the possibility to express themselves. Of the fingers, the pinkie illustrates this point. Of the four fingers it has the biggest range of sideways movement. This is reflected on classical instruments, for instance various flutes and the recorder, where this finger is used to reach two or more holes side-by-side. But for some reason it has never been given any special role in usual electronic interfaces. Rethinking this on a touchscreen interface, the smallest finger should become the most important for sliding things around, maybe only rivaled by the thumb.

Ornaments in music require rapid finger movement. The parergon of speed. The thrills of the flute or the fiddle. Where does the main line end and the ornaments begin? Is the quality of the sound itself also ornamental? This is an instrument for the ornamental alone.

Espen Sommer Eide

Espen Sommer Eide[2] (Tromsø, 1972) is a musician and artist currently living in Bergen. He composes under the alias Phonophani, and as a member of the band Alog. Live he uses elaborate setups of custom made instruments, hybrids combining electronic and acoustic elements. He has several releases on the record label Rune Grammofon. Alog's album Miniatures was awarded the Norwegian Grammy-award (Spellemannprisen) in 2006. In addition to touring extensively with his musical projects, Eide also has produced a series of site-specific pieces and artworks, and is currently a member of the theatre-collective Verdensteatret, involved especially with building instruments and sound design.

Other works include composing and performing music for the 50-year anniversary of Le Corbusiers chapel in Ronchamp, France, building the sound art installation Sonus Barentsicus for the Northern Lights Festival in Tromsø, Norway, and a special performance at the Manifesta7 biennale in Italy, where local vinyl records were reconstructed into new musical instruments. Recently he presented the work Kreken, made for a custom built instrument, the "concertinome", at the GRM festival Presénces Electronique in Paris. Eide has also been involved in a series of net-art projects with various topics connected to the Barents and arctic regions of Northern Norway, under the heading of "rural readers", including a permanent installation for the Eastern Sami Museum in Neiden, Norway. In addition to making music and art, Eide has also been directing the Trollofon electronic music festival in Bergen (2001-2006), and works as artistic developer at BEK (Bergen Center of Electronic Arts).

---

[2] http://sommer.alog.net

Akousmaflore

Each plant in this interactive installation reacts in a different way to human contact or warmth by producing a specific sound. The plant "language" or song occurs through touch and the close proximity of the spectator. The invisible electrical aura of humans acts on the plant branches and encourages them to react. The plants sing when the audience is touching or stroking them lightly. A plant concert is created.

In their artwork, the artists Scenocosme create hybrids between plants and digital technology. Plants are natural sensors and are sensitive to various energy flows. Digital technologies permit us to establish a relationship between plants and sound. This work displays the effects of random data flow and plant interaction. The data is modified as the spectator meanders around and touches the installation, resulting in a random musical universe. The audience's gestures and movements generate sound effects and change the texture of the sound.

The human body continually produces an electrical and heat aura in our immediate vicinity, which we cannot feel. In their research, the "design of the invisible", the artists' approach is to animate that which we cannot detect. Mixing reality with imagination, they propose a sensory experience that encourage the audience to think about our relationship with other living things and with energy. Indoor plants can have an ambiguous existence, on the one hand as decorative object and on the other hand as living being. It is said that "inanimate objects" can react when they receive human attention. Through *Akousmaflore*, plants let us know about their existence by a scream, a melody or an acoustical vibration.

The sounds created by the interaction between the ten plants in the installation and the audience are processed on a (hidden) computer and displayed by 5.1 surround sound speakers that are located above the plants.

Gregory Lasserre and Anaïs met den Ancxt

A duo, better known as Scenocosme[3]. They use interactive art, music and architecture. With multiple forms of expression, they invite spectators to be in the centre of musical or choreographic collective performances. Gregory and Anaïs also explore invisible relationships with our environment: they can feel energetic variations of living beings, and they design interactive stagings where spectators share sensory and amazing experiences.

The artists have exhibited their interactive installation artworks at ZKM (Germany), Villa Romana of Firenze (Italy), Museum Art Gallery of Nova Scotia (Canada) and in many international biennals and festivals : BIACS3 - Biennale of contemporary art in Sevilla (Spain), INDAF (Korea), Experimenta (Australia), C.O.D.E (Canada), ISEA (Belfast), Futuresonic (UK), WRO (Poland), FAD (Brasil), Citysonics (Belgium), Ososphere, EXIT, VIA, Scopitone, Seconde-nature (France), in various art centers : Kibla (Slovenia), Utsikten Kunstsenter (Norway), Centre des arts d'Enghien-les-Bains (France), and many more.

---

[3] http://www.scenocosme.com

Auditory Augmentation at your Fingertips

Everybody is talking about augmented reality nowadays: the increasingly popular technology which presents additional information about the environment through the use of visual overlays on camera-equipped phones. But our realities are also full of sound, sound that can be digitally augmented to communicate information and create feelings. What kind of information about our surroundings can be communicated by modifying the sounds made by common objects that we interact with? This is the question addressed in the practice of auditory augmentation.

In this exhibit, the visitor is able to experience how a workplace common soundscape may be artificially augmented with information streams a possible worker might be interested in. By carefully altering the structure-borne sound of a keyboard, which here stands for an everyday computer interface, information on the current weather situation is overlaid to the environmental soundscape. This auditory augmentation alters according to the readings of environmental sensors. The worker therefore gets a subliminally perceived hint about the current weather conditions outside his office. Adding an auditory augmentation to structure-borne sounds means to insert a thin layer between people's action and an object's natural auditory re-action. This auditory augmentation is designed to be easily overlaid to existing sounds while it does not change prominent and, perception-wise, essential auditory features of the augmented objects. In a peripheral monitoring situation as it can be found at a workplace, the data representation therefore tends to be below the user's conscious perception. A characteristic change in the data stream, however, will likely claim user attention. The exhibited setup shows the capabilities of auditory augmentaion at hand of characteristic values for several weather situations. The visitor can switch between these setups and experience the difference of the changing keyboard sonic character.

René Tünnermann, Till Bovermann, and Thomas Hermann

René Tünnermann is a research associate of the Ambient Intelligence Group at the Cognitive Interaction Technology Center of Excellence at Bielefeld University (CITEC). He studied science informatics at Bielefeld University. During his studies he worked as a student worker at the Neuroinformatics Group of Bielefeld University and at the project CRC673 – Alignment in Communication. His research focus lies with tangible interfaces and interactive surfaces.

Till Bovermann is a researcher, artist, and engineer currently exploring tangible and auditory interfaces as a researcher at the Media Lab Helsinki, where he leads the TAI Studio. He has worked at various institutes within Bielefeld University, Germany, and most recently in the Ambient Intelligence Group of the CITEC Cognitive Interaction Technology Center of Excellence. He has also taught at the Institute for Music and Media of the University of Music Düsseldorf and at UdK Berlin. His professional background is in Computer Science with a focus on Robotics. He received his PhD developing tangible auditory interfaces[4]. Till Boverman's artistic works are mostly concerned with the relationship between digital and physical space. He is co-founder of TooManyGadgets, a media art group that tries to illuminate this relationship. Their most recent project "...between..." was exhibited at the Nacht der Klänge at Bielefeld University. In addition to his work with TooManyGadgets, Till has created installation pieces in conjunction with Animax, Bonn. Alongside his artistic and academic work, Till also develops software, mainly in SuperCollider.

Thomas Hermann studied physics at Bielefeld University. From 1998 to 2001 he was a member of the interdisciplinary Graduate Program "Task-oriented Communication". He started the research on sonification and auditory display in the Neuroinformatics Group and received a Ph.D. in Computer Science in 2002 from Bielefeld University (thesis: Sonification for Exploratory Data Analysis). After research stays at the Bell Labs (NJ, USA, 2000) and GIST (Glasgow University, UK, 2004), he is currently assistant professor and head of the Ambient Intelligence Group within CITEC, the Center of Excellence in Cognitive Interaction Technology, Bielefeld University. His research focus is sonification, datamining, human-computer interaction and cognitive interaction technology.

---

[4] http://tangibleauditoryinterfaces.de/index.php/tai-applications/auditory-augmentation/

aura: the stuff that forms around you

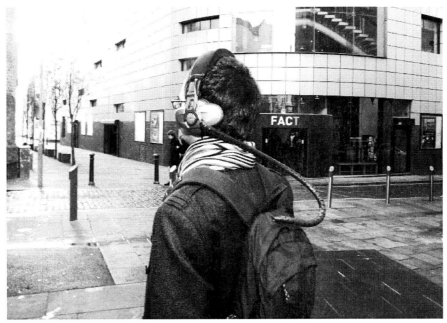

aura is a located sound project that explores notions of consumption and ownership by allowing users to effect an audio landscape as they move within the real world. Each exploration of the outdoor area near the gallery is tracked by GPS and layered onto recordings of all previous explorations. This map is used to generate surround sounds that result from landscape erosion.

Imagine a playing field after a fresh falling of snow. The snow lies evenly and untrodden. This represents an empty *aura* sound world, which would sound like soft pink noise, balanced with a gently undulating hum. Someone walks across the field leaving footprints, the snow is sullied, eroded, the walker has left a patina in the world. In the *aura* world this patina is first represented by shifts in the intensity and changes in filtering, the audio moving as the explorer crosses the footprints. As more people walk in the world the sound becomes more and more fragmented and distorted, leaving smaller and smaller pockets of unconsumed beauty.

aura was premiered at the _enter festival, Cambridge, UK in April 2007 and has been exhibited at Ding Dong, FACT, Liverpool and ISEA09, Belfast.

Steve Symons

A sound artist[5] known for an innovative series of sonic augmented reality projects titled *aura* and as a member of the award winning Owl Project. He creates digital systems for his own use, which are often released for artists and musicians as free and open-source tools, and is currently extending this process to include commissioning artists to make new content for the systems he has created, thus challenging traditional notions of artist, maker and producer. These activities operate under the guise of muio.org, an art and technology interface consultancy he set up to facilitate his artistic practice and exploit the technology created in its realisation.

Owl Project is a three person collaboration (Steve Symons, Simon Blackmore and Anthony Hall) who make and perform with sculptural sonic interfaces that critique human desire for technology. Nominated for the Northern Art Prize and awarded the Best of Manchester 2009, Owl Project (along with production manager Ed Carter) hold one of the "Artists Taking the Lead" commissions as part of the Cultural Olympiad.

---

[5] http://stevesymons.net/

Crush–2

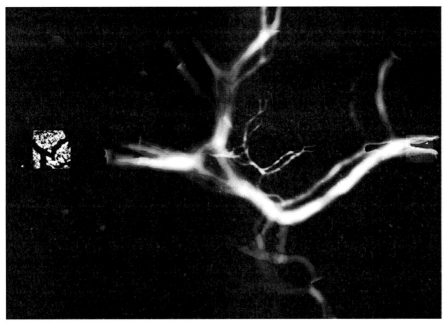

An interactive sound-art installation exploring the microscopic forces released during the process of crushing rock. The installation draws from two research projects at PGP (Physics of Geological Processes in Oslo): 3D numerical simulations of grain fracture and fault gouge evolution during shear (Steffen Abe and Karen Mair), and the study of real acoustic emissions from granite, basalt and sandstone under compression (Alexandre Schubnel).

Crush involves 3D electroacoustic sound, a loudspeaker array, wireless headphones, a motion tracking system, still images and a real-time video projection. In this installation, the audience can move through a virtual, immersive space, experiencing the dynamics of deformation from "inside" the rock.

Work on Crush began with the accurate sonification of data from simulations and real acoustic emissions. Subsequent stages involved degrees of abstraction through the choice of sound material, data mapping rules, interaction design and material montage. In the final work, micro-scale processes are enlarged into a dynamic system audible through sound color (timbre), texture, shape and spatial geometry.

Natasha Barrett

Natasha Barrett[6] has performed and has been commissioned throughout the world. She has collaborated with well-known ensembles, scientists and designers, electronic performance groups and festivals. Her output spans concert composition through to sound-art, often incorporates latest technologies and includes a major work for the Norwegian state commission for art in public spaces. Barrett holds an MA and PhD from Birmingham and City University, London. Both degrees were funded by the humanities section of the British Academy. Since 1999 Norway has been her compositional and research base for an international platform. Her composition has received numerous recognitions, most notably the Nordic Council Music Prize (2006).

---

[6] http://www.natashabarrett.org

MindBox

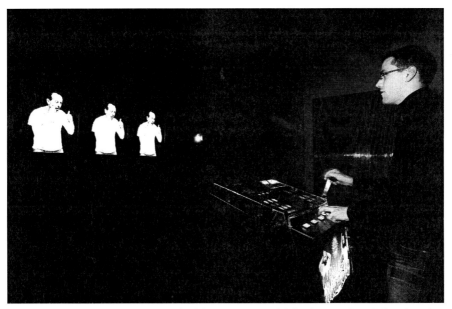

An intuitive audiovisual musical instrument, which aims to break barriers between players, performers and audience. The media slot machine allows for musical re-interpretation of sounds and images. It gives access to expressive parameters while at the same time preserving the character of the pre-recorded performance material. There are two choices for the audience: They can either let the instrument autonomously generate variations, or they can interact with the installation and take over the audio-visual and musical control. Players can stay in a consistent and continuous flow while switching between both modes. The installation is based on the artist's H.RP or 'Humatic Re-Performing' concept.

The intuitive interface of the vintage slot machine, the music-video style beatboxer, and the playful, tactile interaction engage the audience while playing or observing the installation.

Christian Graupner, Roberto Zappalà, Norbert Schnell, and Nils Peters

Christian Graupner is a Berlin-based artist, film composer, and guest artist at ZKM Karlsruhe. His earlier works include drawings and experimental electronic music. In 2000 he and Nils Peters formed the independent artist group and production company Humatic[7]. In his latest work, Christian explores the practices and myths around

---

[7] http://www.humatic.de/cv/cg.html

pop and contemporary music . He combines multiscreen videos and multichannel sound with mechanisms that are partly controlled by machines and partly user-controlled *humatic* interfaces and mechanisms. His recent sculptural/media work includes gambling machines and asian mojo figures, feedback guitars and beatbox-like vocal and dance performances. In processing visual and audio material, he uses and adapts available computer programs, but also uses software coded by his project collaborators. His work has been shown and performed worldwide.

Roberto Zappalà founded the Compagnia Zappalà Danza in 1989 to widen and deepen his own research in choreography. Since then, he has created more than 25 pieces that have been presented throughout Europe, South America and the Middle East. He is the artistic director of the Scenario Pubblico performing arts center in Catania, Sicily.

Norbert Schnell studied telecommunications and music, and worked at the Graz Institut für Elektronische Musik (IEM) as a developer and projects adviser. In 1995 he joined the Real-Time Systems team at IRCAM (Institut de Recherche et Coordination Acoustique/Musique) in Paris. He is involved in international scientific and artistic projects. In 2006 he chaired the NIME conference.

Nils Peters is a software artist. Starting off with music, his work has taken him to fields such as installation, theater and performance. He joined machinery art ensembles such as Dead Chickens and BBM, where he combined music and robot sequencing. With Humatic he developed a patented realtime multimedia sequencing environment. He received several grants for his projects. His musical work has been published by the Academy of Arts, Berlin.

SonicChair

The interactive sonification of tacTiles used on an office chair can provide auditory feedback that triggers users to be more dynamic and flexible on the chair. This application of tacTiles is an interactive office chair that reacts to the movements of the office worker. The sonification of the chair user's movements could help reducing back problems in office work contexts.

TacTiles [52] are wireless modular tactile sensitive surface elements that can be laid on the floor or furniture and can be used for a variety of applications. They can be used as interface for human-computer interaction or ambient information systems. The system can be used for real-time sonification, for process monitoring and biofeedback. Future applications could include pairing tacTiles with sonification for games.

Thomas Hermann and Risto Kõiva

Thomas Hermann studied physics at Bielefeld University. From 1998 to 2001 he was a member of the interdisciplinary Graduate Program "Task-oriented Communication". He started the research on sonification and auditory display in the Neuroinformatics Group and received a Ph.D. in Computer Science in 2002 from Bielefeld University (thesis: Sonification for Exploratory Data Analysis). After research stays at the Bell Labs (NJ, USA, 2000) and GIST (Glasgow University, UK, 2004), he is currently assistant professor and head of the Ambient Intelligence Group within CITEC, the Center of Excellence in Cognitive Interaction Technology, Bielefeld University. His research focus is sonification, datamining, human-computer interaction and cognitive interaction technology.

Risto Kõiva studied at the Faculty of Information Technology of the Tallinn Technical University (Estonia), where he received in 2000 a diploma in Computer Control and Automation (with honors). After some years of experience in industry, he is currently pursuing a PhD program in Computer Science at the Neuroinformatics Group (AG Neuroinformatik) of the Bielefeld University. His fields of interest are sensorics, robotics and computer control. Concurrently he is responsible for the Center of Excellence in Cognitive Interaction Technology, Bielefeld University (CITEC) workshop. In his spare time he is an excited R/C modeler, mostly interested in helicopters.

Klanghelm / Sonic Helmet

Our experience of sound is not only about hearing and listening. *Klanghelm / Sonic Helmet* is a wearable sonic object, intended to be worn on the head. A three-channel sound system creates an intimate three-dimensional sound field and vibro-tactile stimuli on the skull. Several sound artists and electroacoustic musicians have contributed their compositions for the *Sonic Helmet*.

This work deals with the issue of intersensory sonic perception. It is more an object than an installation, as the object itself creates the audio-tactile sonic experience without the sound being mediated into the surrounding space. The Sonic Helmet enables the audience to experience sound composition through the sense of hearing as well as through the sense of touch. The sound is played just next to the ears and this vibroacoustic stimulation is mediated directly through the skull. The *Sonic Helmet* could be called a true "headphone", as it involves the whole head, in three dimensions. Overall, the vibroacoustic stimulation supports another layer of sonic reality.

Satoshi Morita

Satoshi Morita (Tokyo, 1974) deals with the issue of "bodily listening" in his practice, and focusses on multimodal aspects of sound, which involve auditory and tactile perception. A series of sonic objects produced by him create a multi-modal sonic experience of the inner (kinesthetic) and outer (auditory) spaces of the body.

The multi-channel sound system used in Satoshi's work provides tactile stimuli by vibrotactile transducers on different locations of the body. Sound materials for the sonic objects are composed to gain corporeal sensitivity for audio-tactile perception regarding musical parameters such as frequency, intensity, rhythm, etc.

His experience at different artist-in-residence programs gave him opportunities to observe the diversity and uniqueness of sound in the environment, for instance as Nodar artist in residence in Portugal (2009). Satoshi's works won several prizes, such as a Honorary Mention from Prix Ars Electronica (2008). His works have been exhibited internationally including; BIORHYTHM - Music and the Body, Dublin, 2010; Sound Travels, NAISA, Toronto, 2010; Device_art 3.010, Tokyo, 2010; Kapelica Gallery, Ljubljana, 2010; CyberArts - Ars Electronica, Linz, 2008; paraflows, Vienna, 2008; Touch Me Festival, Zagreb, 2008.

Swinging Suitcase

Each *Swinging Suitcase* consists of a vintage hard-shelled suitcase containing accelerometers, microprocessors and flash memory cards containing short sparrow vocalizations. When a suitcase is picked up, the birds begin to make noise, which calibrates to reflect movement - accelerating and multiplying in response to the gesture of the user.

The vocalizations in the *Swinging Suitcase* are constructed from sixty different source clips of house sparrows, which are arranged into responses that range from single chirps to social chatter to scolding. As the suitcase is swung, the tracks are played in relationship to how the suitcase is being moved and for how long.

While we understand that machines do not have feelings, if an event occurs that triggers a deeply ingrained social behavior, we will automatically respond according to the ingrained social conventions that we know. In the case of the *Swinging Suitcase*, reciprocal behavior is triggered through a user's initial encounter with the piece: grasping and lifting the suitcase is intuitive. However, when the user picks up the piece, the first bird chirrups. An everyday action triggers a sound that is instantly recognizable - and this triggers the suspension of disbelief and an almost universal sense of delight. Since we know that most birds are small, it is plausible that there is a bird inside the suitcase.

The piece is designed to be "just intuitive enough" - while the "birds" do "respond" to motion and gesture, there is still a layer of unpredictability in the interaction model that helps to anthropomorphize the piece, and to create a reciprocal dialogue between body, artwork and site. Interaction becomes confounded when the gestures of the user become repetitive and the vocalizations become more complex - the "birds" become restless, and as you play the birds, the birds play you.

By bringing birds through different places, especially those places where birds should not be, the *Swinging Suitcase* may initiate dialogues with passersby, shift the acoustic ecologies of shared public spaces, or be used for performative intervention, trickery, or play.

Jessica Thompson

Jessica Thompson[8] (Toronto, 1975) is a new media artist whose projects facilitate social interaction within public space through sound, performance and mobile technologies. Her work has been shown in exhibitions and festivals such as Art Basel Miami Beach; ISEA 2006, San Jose, CA; FINE/LINE, Denmark; the Conflux Festival, New York; Thinking Metropolis, Copenhagen; (in) visible Cities, Winnipeg; Beyond/In Western New York, Buffalo; and the Deep Wireless Festival of Radio and Transmission Art, Toronto. Her projects have appeared in publications such as Canadian Art, c Magazine, Acoustic Territories, and numerous art and technology blogs. In 2011, Thompson will be a Senior Artist at Recycling Pervasive Media, Intervening in Planned Obsolescence and Practicing Technological Sustainability, a workshop hosted by the Banff Centre for the Arts.

---

[8] http://jessicathompson.ca

Random Access Lattice

An installation allowing one person to interactively explore a virtual sonic sculpture constructed from speech recordings, arranged in a three-dimensional lattice structure. The time axes of the recordings are aligned with the extent of virtual slabs arranged orthogonally in the three Cartesian dimensions and permeating each other. The lattice is formed by 625 slabs, holding almost two hours of speech recordings of a large variety of languages on more than 1.5 km of virtual tape.

One audience member may explore the stored texts by moving a small hand-held loudspeaker through the lattice. The motion-tracked speaker acts as playback head of a virtual tape recorder where the tape is not stored on reels but arranged in a three-dimensional weave. The *Random Access Lattice* is inspired by Nam June Paik's installation Random Access Memory (1963) where magnetic tape was glued to a gallery wall and could be played back by sliding a hand-held playback head over the tape - a prominent historic example of sonic interaction design in the arts.

When moving steadily and exactly along one lattice axis in the right direction, a speech recording may be played back accurately. But, as the rigidity of the Cartesian lattice structure opposes itself against the free movement of the hand, the trajectory of the hand is very likely to traverse several slabs und thus create a new utterance, formed by fragments of different recordings strung together. Since body movements may easily be repeated and slightly varied, a situation is created that allows for a playful and intuitive (embodied) exploration of this interactive sonic sculpture.

The *Random Access Lattice* is based on the experiences gained in the Embodied Generative Music project[9], which studied phenomena of embodiment in sound production by means of touch-less interfaces. Arrangements similar to the *Random Access Lattice* have been developed and explored in the project. A prototype of the

---

[9] http://embodiedgenerativemusic.org

Tracked Hand-held Speaker (THS) used in the installation has been explored in a WG3 meeting[10] of the SID COST action in Graz in May 2009.

Gerhard Eckel

Gerhard Eckel (Vienna, 1962), Composer and Sound Artist, since 2005 Professor of Computer Music and Multimedia at the Institute of Electronic Music and Acoustics, University of Music and Performing Arts Graz. Studies in musicology and electronic music composition in Vienna. 1989-1996 artistic researcher at IRCAM, Pompidou Centre, Paris; 1996-2005 research scientist at Fraunhofer Institute for Media Communication, Bonn; composer in residence at the Banff Centre for the Arts in 1995 and 2000; current artistic research projects: Embodied Generative Music, The Choreography of Sound.

---

[10] http://sid-musicart.wikispaces.com/THS

Thicket

The iPad application *Thicket*[11] is an audiovisual world of texture, movement, line and tone. By drawing on the screen with your fingers, you create dense, mesmerizing sonic and visual patterns within a space of warm, bright, rhythmic sound design and constantly evolving, bending, elegant scrawls.

Thicket has a single, unified gestural interface for controlling both sound and picture. There are no knobs, sliders, or buttons. *Thicket* aims to be expressive and intuitive, working with the grain of the touch screen interface, and moving away from the point and click paradigm of traditional software interfaces. *Thicket* is not a tool, it is a piece of art. Therefore, *Thicket* is not open-ended, and guides the user strongly toward a particular audio and visual aesthetic. *Thicket*'s basic sound and visual palette are fixed, but the user has the freedom to explore within these fixed palettes.

Joshue Ott and Morgan Packard

Audio-visual duo Joshue Ott and Morgan Packard's work, while often quite abstract, daring and experimental, is informed by the discipline, structure, and craft of their former study in more traditional art forms - figurative drawing, classical harmony and counterpoint, theater, jazz improvisation. The result is an immersive, engrossing multi-sensory experience with fascinating strength and agility.

Over the past several years, both Ott and Packard have emerged as exciting new voices in the experimental electronica and live cinema scenes, both as indi-

---

[11] http://apps.intervalstudios.com/thicket/

vidual artists and as a collaborative duo. Recent highlights include performances at prestigious festivals: Mutek (Montreal, Canada), Plateaux (Torun, Poland), Communikey (Boulder, Colorado), a collaborative DVD release: Unsimulatable, and an iPhone/iPad app: Thicket.

KII - Voicetopological Interface

KII (Kempelen 2.0) is a voice-topological interface for gestural navigation in linguistic space. The hands serve as speech organ during the articulation process. By using sensors, the device determines how open both hands are, their position in space, their relative height. These and other parameters are then assigned to the jaw and tongue position in the mouth as well as to pitch and rhythm. Phoneme production is based on phonetic laws. Through the implementation of musical scales and speech rhythms, a spoken language is produced. Their context of meaning is not characterized by the conveyance of information but by the abstraction of the voice in the tonal linguistic space. Articulatory-topological phonetics deals with the speech process - parts of the body serve as speech organs during the articulation process. It is therefore historically linked to Kempelen's motif of speech generation for the voiceless: voice generation for the speechless.

When we speak or sing, we typically also produce other articulations of various body parts, such as gestures. The artist's research focuses on these articulations of behaviour, posture and expression that are part of human speech. This work does not aim to reproduce meaning as source of communication, but to generate behaviour by interaction. The electronic voice is not intended to imitate, but to be an instrument. To distinguish this work from original speech, no original voices are used. Instead, high quality realtime speech synthesizers create the voices.

Michael Markert

Michael Markert[12] is a media-artist and musician specializing in programming and electronics. He lives in Nuremberg, Germany. His research in intuitive musical interfaces started with a diploma in Multimedia and Communications Design. Since then, he has developed various interactive sensory devices which he has used for installations and as musical instruments. His work focuses on exploring harmonic musical control through intuitive realtime sensory processing and cybernetic interaction systems, thereby overruling hierarchic mechanisms of reception in art.

Since 2005 he has been a member of the Urban Research Institute for Public Art and Urban Ethology (Intermedia), founded by Georg Winter. In 2008 he graduated with a second diploma at the College of Fine Arts Nuremberg and is currently teaching at the College of Fine Arts in Nuremberg and at the Bauhaus University Weimar, in the Faculty of Media.

---

[12] http://www.audiocommander.de

References

1. D. Arfib, J.-J. Filatriau, and L. Kessous. Prototyping musical experiments for Tangisense, a tangible and traceable table. In *Proc. Sound and Music Computing Conf.*, pages 247–252, Porto, Portugal, 2009.
2. S. Bakker, R. van den Berg, S. Pijnappel, and E. van den Hoven. Sounds like home: Sonification and physical interaction in the periphery and center of attention. In *Human Interaction with Auditory Displays – Proc. Interactive Sonification Workshop*, pages 55–58, 2010.
3. B. Bank and M. Karjalainen. Passive admittance matrix modeling for guitar synthesis. In *Proc. Conf. on Digital Audio Effects*, pages 3–8, Graz, Austria, 2010.
4. B. Bank, S. Zambon, and F. Fontana. A modal-based real-time piano synthesizer. *IEEE Transactions on Audio, Speech and Language Processing*, 18:809–821, May 2010.
5. J. Bardzell, J. Bolter, and J. Löwgren. Interaction criticism: three readings of an interaction design, and what they get us. *Interactions*, 17(2):32–37, 2010.
6. S. Barrass, N. Schaffert, and T. Barrass. Probing preferences between six designs of interactive sonifications for recreational sports, health and fitness. In *Human Interaction with Auditory Displays – Proc. Interactive Sonification Workshop*, pages 23–30, 2010.
7. J. Bensoam, R. Caussé, C. Vergez, N. Misdariis, and N. Ellis. Sound synthesis for three-dimensional object: dynamic contact between two arbitrary elastic bodies. In *Proc. Stockholm Music Acoustics Conf.*, pages 369–372, 2003.
8. F. Bevilacqua, B. Zamborlin, A. Sypniewski, N. Schnell, F. Guédy, and N. Rasamimanana. Continuous realtime gesture following and recognition. In S. Kopp and I. Wachsmuth, editors, *Gesture in Embodied Communication and Human-Computer Interaction*, volume 5934 of *Lecture Notes in Computer Science*, pages 73–84. Springer Berlin / Heidelberg, 2010.
9. T. Bianco, V. Freour, N. Rasamimanana, F. Bevilaqua, and R. Caussé. On gestural variation and coarticulation effects in sound control. In S. Kopp and I. Wachsmuth, editors, *Gesture in Embodied Communication and Human-Computer Interaction*, volume 5934 of *Lecture Notes in Computer Science*, pages 134–145. Springer Berlin / Heidelberg, 2010.
10. E. Brazil. A review of methods and frameworks for sonic interaction design: Exploring existing approaches. In S. Ystad, M. Aramaki, R. Kronland-Martinet, and K. Jensen, editors, *Auditory Display*, volume 5954 of *Lecture Notes in Computer Science*, pages 41–67. Springer Berlin / Heidelberg, 2010.
11. R. Bresin, A. de Witt, S. Papetti, M. Civolani, and F. Fontana. Expressive sonification of footstep sounds. In *Human Interaction with Auditory Displays – Proc. Interactive Sonification Workshop*, pages 51–54, 2010.
12. R. Bresin, S. Delle Monache, F. Fontana, S. Papetti, P. Polotti, and Y. Visell. Auditory feedback through continuous control of crumpling sound synthesis. In *Proc. CHI Workshop on Sonic Interaction Design*, pages 23–28, Florence, Italy, 2008.
13. W. Buxton. *Sketching user experiences: getting the design right and the right design*. Morgan Kaufmann Pub, San Francisco, CA, 2007.

14. S. Canazza, A. Rodà, and D. Salvati. A microphone array approach for browsable sound-scapes. In *Proc. Colloquio di Informatica Musicale*, Torino, Italy, 2010.
15. B. Caramiaux, F. Bevilacqua, and N. Schnell. Towards a gesture-sound cross-modal analysis. In S. Kopp and I. Wachsmuth, editors, *Gesture in Embodied Communication and Human-Computer Interaction*, volume 5934 of *Lecture Notes in Computer Science*, pages 158–170. Springer Berlin / Heidelberg, 2010.
16. G. Caridakis, K. Karpouzis, M. Wallace, L. Kessous, and N. Amir. Multimodal user's affective state analysis in naturalistic interaction. *Journal on Multimodal User Interfaces*, 3:49–66, 2010.
17. M. Civolani and F. Fontana. A nonlinear digital model of the EMS VCS3 voltage-controlled filter. In *Proc. Conf. on Digital Audio Effects*, pages 35–42, Helsinki, Finland, 2008.
18. J. Cordeiro. pDaniM: A case study on interactive processes for expressive music generation in the computer animation production pipeline. In *Proc. Int. Conf. on Digital Arts*, pages 233–238, Porto, Portugal, 2008.
19. J. Cordeiro and N. Makelberge. Hurly Burly: An experimental framework for sound based social networking. In *Proc. Int. Conf. on Auditory Display*, Paris, France, 2010.
20. E. Costanza and J. Huang. Designable visual markers. In *Proc. Int. Conf. on Human factors in computing systems*, pages 1879–1888, New York, NY, 2009. ACM.
21. A. Crevoisier. Future-instruments.net: Towards the creation of hybrid electronic-acoustic musical instruments. In *Proc. CHI Workshop on Sonic Interaction Design*, pages 53–58, Florence, Italy, 2008.
22. Y. De Quay and S. A. v. D. Skogstad. Dance jockey: Performing computer music by dancing. *Leonardo Music Journal*, 2011. To appear.
23. S. Delle Monache, D. Hug, and C. Erkut. Basic exploration of narration and performativity for sounding interactive commodities. In R. Nordahl, S. Serafin, F. Fontana, and S. Brewster, editors, *Haptic and Audio Interaction Design*, volume 6306 of *Lecture Notes in Computer Science*, pages 65–74. Springer Berlin / Heidelberg, 2010.
24. S. Delle Monache, P. Polotti, and D. Rocchesso. A toolkit for explorations in sonic interaction design. In *Proc. Audio Mostly Conf.*, pages 1–7, New York, NY, 2010. ACM.
25. S. Dimitrov, M. Alonso, and S. Serafin. Developing block-movement, physical-model based objects for the Reactable. In *Proc. Conf. on New Interfaces for Musical Expression*, pages 211–214, Genova, Italy, 2008.
26. N. Diniz, M. Demey, and M. Leman. An interactive framework for multilevel sonification. In *Human Interaction with Auditory Displays – Proc. Interactive Sonification Workshop*, pages 65–68, 2010.
27. J. P. Djajadiningrat, W. W. Gaver, and J. W. Fres. Interaction relabelling and extreme characters: methods for exploring aesthetic interactions. In *Proc. Conf. on Designing Interactive Systems: processes, practices, methods, and techniques*, pages 66–71, New York, NY, 2000. ACM.
28. T. Drori and M. Rinott. Pixel materiali: a system for creating and understanding pixel animations. In *Proc. Int. Conf. on Interaction Design and Children*, pages 157–160, New York, NY, 2007. ACM.
29. G. Dubus and R. Bresin. Sonification of sculler movements, development of preliminary methods. In *Human Interaction with Auditory Displays – Proc. Interactive Sonification Workshop*, pages 39–43, 2010.
30. I. Ekman and M. Rinott. Using vocal sketching for designing sonic interactions. In *Proc. Conf. on Designing Interactive Systems*, pages 123–131, New York, NY, 2010. ACM.
31. C. Erkut, J.-J. Filatriau, R. Lehembre, and I. Ekman. Sonic interaction design with physiological interfaces in a workshop setting. In *Proc. CHI Workshop on Sonic Interaction Design*, pages 47–52, Florence, Italy, 2008.
32. K. Falkenberg Hansen and M. Alonso. More DJ techniques on the Reactable. In *Proc. Conf. on New Interfaces for Musical Expression*, pages 207–210, Genova, Italy, 2008.
33. K. Falkenberg Hansen, M. Alonso, and S. Dimitrov. Combining DJ scratching, tangible interfaces and a physics-based model of friction sounds. In *Proc. Int. Computer Music Conf.*, volume 2, pages 45–48, 2007.

34. K. Falkenberg Hansen and R. Bresin. The Skipproof virtual turntable for high-level control of scratching. *Computer Music Journal*, 34(2):39–50, 2010.

35. K. Falkenberg Hansen, M. Fabiani, and R. Bresin. Analysis of the acoustics and playing strategies of turntable scratching. *Acta Acustica united with Acustica*, 97:303–314(12), March/April 2011.

36. A. Farnell. *Designing Sound*. MIT Press, Cambridge, MA, 2010.

37. J.-J. Filatriau and D. Arfib. Creation and exploration of a perceptual sonic textures space using a tangible interface. In *Proc. Sound and Music Computing Conf.*, Barcelona, Spain, 2010.

38. F. Fontana and M. Civolani. Modeling of the EMS VCS3 voltage-controlled filter as a nonlinear filter network. *IEEE Transactions on Audio, Speech and Language Processing*, 18:760–772, May 2010.

39. K. Franinovic, L. Gaye, and F. Behrendt. Exploring sonic interaction with artifacts in everyday contexts. In *Proc. Int. Conf. on Auditory Display*, Paris, France, 2008.

40. K. Franinovic, D. Hug, and Y. Visell. Sound embodied: Explorations of sonic interaction design for everyday objects in a workshop setting. In *Proc. Int. Conf. on Auditory Display*, Montreal, Canada, 2007.

41. C. Frauenberger and T. Stockman. Auditory display design – an investigation of a design pattern approach. *International Journal of Human-Computer Studies*, 67(11):907 – 922, 2009. Special issue on Sonic Interaction Design.

42. J. Gampe. Interactive narration within audio augmented realities. In I. Iurgel, N. Zagalo, and P. Petta, editors, *Interactive Storytelling*, volume 5915 of *Lecture Notes in Computer Science*, pages 298–303. Springer Berlin / Heidelberg, 2009.

43. R. I. Godøy, A. R. Jensenius, and K. Nymoen. Chunking in music by coarticulation. *Acta Acustica united with Acustica*, 96:690–700(11), July/August 2010.

44. R. I. Godøy and M. Leman. *Musical gestures: Sound, movement, and meaning*. Routledge, New York, NY, 2010.

45. S. Goto. netBody. In *ACM SIGGRAPH ASIA – Art Gallery & Emerging Technologies: Adaptation*, pages 20–20, New York, NY, 2009. ACM.

46. S. Goto and R. Powell. netBody - "Augmented Body and Virtual Body II" with the System, BodySuit, Powered Suit and Second Life – Its introduction of an application of the system. In *Proc. Conf. on New Interfaces for Musical Expression*, pages 48–49, Pittsburgh, PA, 2009.

47. F. Grond and F. Dall'Antonia. Sumo. a sonification utility for molecules. In *Proc. Int. Conf. on Auditory Display*, Paris, France, 2008.

48. F. Grond, T. Hermann, V. Verfaille, and M. Wanderley. Methods for effective sonification of clarinetists' ancillary gestures. In S. Kopp and I. Wachsmuth, editors, *Gesture in Embodied Communication and Human-Computer Interaction*, volume 5934 of *Lecture Notes in Computer Science*, pages 171–181. Springer Berlin / Heidelberg, 2010.

49. F. Grond, S. Janssen, S. Schirmer, and T. Hermann. Browsing RNA structures by interactive sonification. In *Human Interaction with Auditory Displays – Proc. Interactive Sonification Workshop*, pages 11–16, 2010.

50. T. Großhauser and T. Hermann. Multimodal closed-loop human machine interaction. In *Human Interaction with Auditory Displays – Proc. Interactive Sonification Workshop*, pages 59–63, 2010.

51. T. Hermann. Sonic Interaction Design: New applications and challenges for interactive sonification. In *Proc. Conf. on Digital Audio Effects*, Graz, Austria, 2010.

52. T. Hermann and R. Kõiva. tacTiles for ambient intelligence and interactive sonification. In A. Pirhonen and S. Brewster, editors, *Haptic and Audio Interaction Design*, volume 5270 of *Lecture Notes in Computer Science*, pages 91–101. Springer Berlin / Heidelberg, 2008.

53. T. Hermann, J. Neuhoff, and A. Hunt, editors. *The Sonification Handbook*. Logos Verlag, Berlin, Germany, 2011.

54. T. Hermann, Y. Visell, J. Williamson, R. Murray-Smith, and E. Brazil. Sonification for sonic interaction design. In *Proc. CHI Workshop on Sonic Interaction Design*, pages 35–40, Florence, Italy, 2008.

55. D. Hug. Towards a hermeneutics and typology of sound for interactive commodities. In *Proc. CHI Workshop on Sonic Interaction Design*, pages 11–16, Florence, Italy, 2008.

56. D. Hug. Investigating narrative and performative sound design strategies for interactive commodities. In S. Ystad, M. Aramaki, R. Kronland-Martinet, and K. Jensen, editors, *Auditory Display*, volume 5954 of *Lecture Notes in Computer Science*, pages 12–40. Springer Berlin / Heidelberg, 2010.

57. J. Hummel, T. Hermann, C. Frauenberger, and T. Stockman. Interactive sonification of German wheel sports movement. In *Human Interaction with Auditory Displays – Proc. Interactive Sonification Workshop*, pages 17–22, 2010.

58. A. R. Jensenius, K. Nymoen, and R. I. Godøy. A multilayered GDIF-based setup for studying coarticulation in the movements of musicians. In *Proc. Int. Computer Music Conf., Belfast*, pages 743–746, 2008.

59. A. R. Jensenius, M. Wanderley, R. I. Gødoy, and M. Leman. Musical gestures: concepts and methods in research. In R. I. Godøy and M. Leman, editors, *Musical Gestures: Sound, Movement, and Meaning*, pages 12–35. Routledge, New York, NY, 2010.

60. L. Kessous, G. Castellano, and G. Caridakis. Multimodal emotion recognition in speech-based interaction using facial expression, body gesture and acoustic analysis. *Journal on Multimodal User Interfaces*, 3:33–48, 2010.

61. L. B. Kofoed and R. Nordahl. Medialogy - interdisciplinary education challenge with focus on PBL and students' learning. In *Proc. Int. Conf. Problem Based Learning and Active Learning Methodologies*, Sao Paolo, Brazil, 2010.

62. L. Kolbe, R. Tünnermann, and T. Hermann. Growing neural gas sonification model for interactive surfaces. In *Human Interaction with Auditory Displays – Proc. Interactive Sonification Workshop*, pages 47–50, 2010.

63. G. Kramer and B. N. Walker. Sound science: Marking ten international conferences on auditory display. *ACM Transactions on Applied Perception*, 2:383–388, October 2005.

64. M. Lagrange, L. Martins, J. Murdoch, and G. Tzanetakis. Normalized cuts for predominant melodic source separation. *Audio, Speech, and Language Processing, IEEE Transactions on*, 16(2):278–290, feb. 2008.

65. M. Lagrange, G. Scavone, and P. Depalle. Analysis/synthesis of sounds generated by sustained contact between rigid objects. *IEEE Transactions on Audio, Speech, and Language Processing*, 18(3):509–518, march 2010.

66. O. Lähdeoja. An approach to instrument augmentation: the electric guitar. In *Proc. Conf. on New Interfaces for Musical Expression*, Genova, Italy, 2008.

67. O. Lähdeoja, M. Wanderley, and J. Malloch. Instrument augmentation using ancillary gestures for subtle sonic effects. In *Proc. Sound and Music Computing Conf.*, pages 327–330, Porto, Portugal, 2009.

68. B. Laurel. *Computers as theatre*. Addison-Wesley, Reading, MA, 1991.

69. H.-M. Lehtonen. *Analysis, Perception, and Synthesis of the Piano Sound*. PhD thesis, Aalto University, 2010. http://lib.tkk.fi/Diss/2010/isbn9789526034133/.

70. H.-M. Lehtonen, A. Askenfelt, and V. Välimäki. Analysis of the part-pedaling effect in the piano. *The Journal of the Acoustical Society of America*, 126(2):EL49–EL54, 2009.

71. G. Lemaitre, O. Houix, Y. Visell, K. Franinovic, N. Misdariis, and P. Susini. Toward the design and evaluation of continuous sound in tangible interfaces: The Spinotron. *International Journal of Human-Computer Studies*, 67(11):976–993, 2009. Special issue on Sonic Interaction Design.

72. M. Leman. *Embodied music cognition and mediation technology*. MIT Press, Cambridge, MA, 2008.

73. Y.-K. Lim, E. Stolterman, and J. Tenenberg. The anatomy of prototypes: Prototypes as filters, prototypes as manifestations of design ideas. *ACM Transactions on Computer-Human Interaction*, 15(2):1–27, 2008.

74. M. Lopez and S. Pauletto. The design of an audio film for the visually impaired. In *Proc. Int. Conf. on Auditory Display*, Copenhagen, Denmark, 2009.

75. M. J. Lopez and S. Pauletto. The design of an audio film: Portraying story, action and interaction through sound. *The Journal of Music and Meaning*, 8, 2009.

76. M. J. Lopez and S. Pauletto. The sound machine: a study in storytelling through sound design. In *Proc. Audio Mostly Conf.*, pages 9:1–9:8, New York, NY, 2010. ACM.
77. J. Löwgren. Toward an articulation of interaction esthetics. *New Review of Hypermedia and Multimedia*, 15(2):1361–4568, 2009.
78. E. Maestre, M. Blaauw, J. Bonada, E. Guaus, and A. Pérez. Statistical modeling of bowing control applied to violin sound synthesis. *IEEE Transactions on Audio, Speech and Language Processing*, 18:855–871, May 2010.
79. L. Martins, J. Burred, G. Tzanetakis, and M. Lagrange. Polyphonic instrument recognition using spectral clustering. In *Proc. Int. Conf. on Music Information Retrieval*, pages 213–218, Vienna, Austria, 2007.
80. L. Martins, M. Lagrange, and G. Tzanetakis. Modeling grouping cues for auditory scene analysis using a spectral clustering formulation. In W. Wang, editor, *Machine Audition: Principles, Algorithms and Systems*, pages 22–60. IGI Global, 2011.
81. J. McDermott, N. J. L. Griffith, and M. O'Neill. Evolutionary computation applied to sound synthesis. In J. Romero and P. Machado, editors, *The Art of Artificial Evolution*, Natural Computing Series, pages 81–101. Springer Berlin Heidelberg, 2008.
82. A. Minard, P. Susini, N. Misdariis, G. Lemaitre, S. McAdams, and E. Parizet. Environmental sound description: comparison and generalization of 4 timbre studies. In *Proc. CHI Workshop on Sonic Interaction Design*, pages 65–70, Florence, Italy, 2008.
83. B. Moens, L. Van Noorden, and M. Leman. D-Jogger: a multimodal music interface for music selection based on user step frequency. In *Proc. Int. Conf. on Haptic and Audio Interaction Design*, Copenhagen, Denmark, 2010. Poster presentation.
84. L. Naveda, F. Gouyon, C. Guedes, and M. Leman. Multidimensional microtiming in samba music. In *Proc. Brazilian Symposium on Computer Music*, Recife, Brazil, 2009.
85. L. Naveda, F. Gouyon, C. Guedes, and M. Leman. Heightened Awareness through Simulated Movement in Multimedia Performance. *Journal of New Music Research*, 40, 2011. "Accepted for publication".
86. L. V. Nickerson. Interactive sonification of grid-based games. In *Proc. Audio Mostly Conf.*, pages 27–34, Glasgow, UK, 2008.
87. R. Nordahl. Sonic interaction design to enhance presence and motion in virtual environments. In *Proc. CHI Workshop on Sonic Interaction Design*, pages 29–34, Florence, Italy, 2008.
88. R. Nordahl, A. Berrezag, S. Dimitrov, L. Turchet, V. Hayward, and S. Serafin. Preliminary experiment combining virtual reality haptic shoes and audio synthesis. In *Proc. Int. Conf. on Haptics - generating and perceiving tangible sensations: Part II*, EuroHaptics'10, pages 123–129, Berlin, Heidelberg, 2010. Springer-Verlag.
89. R. Nordahl and S. Serafin. Using problem based learning to support transdisciplinarity in an HCI education. In *Proc. Conf. on HCI in Education*, Rome, Italy, 2008.
90. R. Nordahl and S. Serafin. Interdisciplinarity in medialogy with applications to sonic interaction design. In *Proc. Conf. on the Participation in the Broadband Society: The Good, the Bad and the Challenging*, pages 881–887, Copenhagen, Denmark, 2009. COST Office.
91. R. Nordahl, S. Serafin, and O. Timcenko. Contextualisation and evaluation of novel sonic interfaces using problem based learning. In *Proc. CHI Workshop on Sonic Interaction Design*, pages 17–22, Florence, Italy, 2008.
92. R. Nordahl, S. Serafin, and L. Turchet. Sound synthesis and evaluation of interactive footsteps for virtual reality applications. In *Virtual Reality Conf.*, pages 147–153, Waltham, MA, march 2010.
93. J. Oliveira, F. Gouyon, L. Martins, and L. Reis. IBT: A Real-time Tempo and Beat Tracking System. In *Proc. Int. Conf. on Music Information Retrieval*, Utrecht, Nederland, 2010.
94. J. Oliveira, L. Naveda, F. Gouyon, M. Leman, and L. Reis. Synthesis of Variable Dancing Styles Based on A Compact Spatiotemporal Representation of Dance. In *Proc. Workshop on Robots and Musical Expressions, IEEE/RSJ Int. Conf. on Intelligent Robots and Systems*, Taipei, Taiwan, 2010.
95. A. Oulasvirta, E. Kurvinen, and T. Kankainen. Understanding contexts by being there: case studies in bodystorming. *Personal and Ubiquitous Computing*, 7:125–134, July 2003.

96. D. Overholt. The musical interface technology design space. *Organised Sound*, 14:217–226, 2009.

97. J. Pakarinen, V. Välimäki, F. Fontana, V. Lazzarini, and J. S. Abel. Recent advances in real-time musical effects, synthesis, and virtual analog models. *EURASIP Journal on Advances in Signal Processing*, 2011. Special issue on musical applications of real-time signal processing.

98. S. Papetti. *Sound modeling issues in interactive sonification - From basic contact events to synthesis and manipulation tools*. PhD thesis, University of Verona, 2010. http://www.di.univr.it/?ent=pubbdip&id=340961&lang=en.

99. S. Papetti, F. Avanzini, and D. Rocchesso. Numerical methods for a non-linear impact model: a comparative study with closed-form corrections. *IEEE Transactions on Audio, Speech and Language Processing*, 19, May 2011. Accepted for publication.

100. S. Pauletto, D. Hug, S. Barrass, and M. Luckhurst. Integrating theatrical strategies into sonic interaction design. In *Proc. Audio Mostly Conf.*, pages 77–82, Glasgow, UK, 2009.

101. S. Pauletto and A. Hunt. Interactive sonification of complex data. *International Journal of Human-Computer Studies*, 67(11):923 – 933, 2009. Special issue on Sonic Interaction Design.

102. C. Picard, C. Frisson, J. Vanderdonckt, D. Tardieu, and T. Dutoit. Towards user-friendly audio creation. In *Proc. Audio Mostly Conf.*, pages 21:1–21:4, New York, NY, 2010. ACM.

103. D. Ploeger. Sonic prosthetics, mediation and performance. In *Theatre Noise Conf.*, London, UK, 2009.

104. D. Ploeger. Heightened awareness through simulated movement in multimedia performance. *Body, Space and Technology Journal*, 9(1), 2010.

105. D. Ploeger. Digital parts / modular doubles: fragmenting the 'digital double'. *Body, Space and Technology Journal*, 10(1), 2011.

106. P. Polotti and C. Benzi. Rhetorical schemes for audio communication. In *Proc. Int. Conf. on Auditory Display*, Paris, France, 2008.

107. P. Polotti and G. Lemaitre. Rhetorical strategies for sound design and auditory display: a case study. *International Journal of Human-Computer Studies*, 2011. Accepted for publication upon revision.

108. P. Polotti and D. Rocchesso. *Sound to sense, sense to sound: a state of the art in sound and music computing*. Logos Verlag, Berlin, Germany, 2008.

109. M. Rath and D. Rocchesso. Continuous sonic feedback from a rolling ball. *IEEE Multimedia*, 12(2):60–69, 2005.

110. M. Reinikainen and T. Björklund. PD6, a method for interdisciplinary product development training and education. In *Proc. SEFI Conf. on Quality Assessment, Employability and Innovation*, Aalborg, Denmark, 2008.

111. M. Reinikainen and T. Björklund. PD6, an idea generation and evaluation method. In *Proc. SEFI Conf. on Quality Assessment, Employability and Innovation*, Aalborg, Denmark, 2008.

112. M. Rinott. The Laughing Swing: Interacting with non-verbal human voice. In *Proc. Int. Conf. on Auditory Display*, Paris, France, 2008. Best Presentation Award.

113. D. Rocchesso and P. Polotti. Designing continuous multisensory interaction. In *Proc. CHI Workshop on Sonic Interaction Design*, pages 3–9, Florence, Italy, 2008.

114. D. Rocchesso, P. Polotti, and S. Delle Monache. Designing continuous sonic interaction. *International Journal of Design*, 3(3), December 2009.

115. D. Rocchesso and S. Serafin. Sonic interaction design. *International Journal of Human-Computer Studies*, 67:905–906, November 2009.

116. D. Rocchesso, S. Serafin, F. Behrendt, N. Bernardini, R. Bresin, G. Eckel, K. Franinovic, T. Hermann, S. Pauletto, P. Susini, and Y. Visell. Sonic interaction design: sound, information and experience. In *CHI Extended abstracts on Human factors in computing systems*, pages 3969–3972, New York, NY, 2008. ACM.

117. S. Ronkainen. User interface sound design for handhelds - case: Internet tablet. In *Proc. CHI Workshop on Sonic Interaction Design*, pages 71–76, Florence, Italy, 2008.

118. C. L. Salter. Dramaturgies of sound: Interactive sound design in live performance. In *Proc. CHI Workshop on Sonic Interaction Design*, pages 41–46, Florence, Italy, 2008.

119. C. L. Salter. *Entangled: Technology and Transformation of Performance*. MIT Press, Cambridge, MA, 2010.

120. C. D. Salvador. A virtual acoustic environment as auditory display front-end for sonification. In *Human Interaction with Auditory Displays – Proc. Interactive Sonification Workshop*, pages 69–72, 2010.

121. D. Salvati and S. Canazza. Improvement of acoustic localization using a short time spectral attenuation with a novel suppression rule. In *Proc. Conf. on Digital Audio Effects*, pages 150–156, Como, Italy, 2009.

122. D. Salvati, A. Rodà, S. Canazza, and G. L. Foresti. A real-time system for multiple acoustic sources localization based on ISP comparison. In *Proc. Conf. on Digital Audio Effects*, pages 201–208, Graz, Austria, 2010.

123. J. C. Schacher. Action and perception in interactive sound installations: An ecological approach. In *Proc. Conf. on New Interfaces for Musical Expression*, Pittsburgh, PA, 2009.

124. J. C. Schacher. Seven years of ICST Ambisonics tools for maxmsp – a brief report. In *Proc. Int. Symposium on Ambisonics and Spherical Acoustics*, Paris, France, 2010.

125. N. Schaffert, K. Matte, and A. O. Effenberg. Listen to the boat motion: acoustic information for elite rowers. In *Human Interaction with Auditory Displays – Proc. Interactive Sonification Workshop*, pages 31–38, 2010.

126. N. Schaffert, K. Mattes, S. Barrass, and A. O. Effenberg. Exploring function and aesthetics in sonifications for elite sports. In R. Dale, D. Burnham, and C. Stevens, editors, *Human Communication Science: A Compendium*, volume 5954 of *ARC Research Network in Human Communication Science*, pages 465–472. Sydney, Australia, 2011.

127. N. Schaffert, K. Mattes, and A. Effenberg. A sound design for acoustic feedback in elite sports. In S. Ystad, M. Aramaki, R. Kronland-Martinet, and K. Jensen, editors, *Auditory Display*, volume 5954 of *Lecture Notes in Computer Science*, pages 143–165. Springer Berlin / Heidelberg, 2010.

128. D. Schleicher, P. Jones, and O. Kachur. Bodystorming as embodied designing. *Interactions*, 17:47–51, November 2010.

129. S. A. v. D. Skogstad and Y. De Quay. Using full body motion capture data as input for musical sound generation. In *Proc. VERDIKT Conf.*, page 67, Oslo, Norway, november 2010.

130. S. A. v. D. Skogstad, K. Nymoen, Y. De Quay, and A. R. Jensenius. OSC implementation and evaluation of the Xsens MVN suit. In *Proc. Int. Conf. on New Interfaces for Musical Expression*, Oslo, Norway, 2011.

131. J. Sterne. *The audible past: Cultural origins of sound reproduction*. Duke University Press, 2003.

132. T. Stockman. Listening to people, objects and interactions. In *Human Interaction with Auditory Displays – Proc. Interactive Sonification Workshop*, pages 3–10, 2010.

133. C. Stoelinga and A. Chaigne. Time-domain modeling and simulation of rolling objects. *Acta Acustica united with Acustica*, 93(2):290–304, 2007.

134. D. Stowell, A. Robertson, N. Bryan-Kinns, and M. Plumbley. Evaluation of live human-computer music-making: Quantitative and qualitative approaches. *International Journal of Human-Computer Studies*, 67(11):960 – 975, 2009. Special issue on Sonic Interaction Design.

135. The S2S2 Consortium. A roadmap for sound and music computing. Technical report, 2007.

136. J. Thompson, J. Kuchera-Morin, M. Novak, D. Overholt, L. Putnam, G. Wakefield, and W. Smith. The Allobrain: An interactive, stereographic, 3D audio, immersive virtual world. *International Journal of Human-Computer Studies*, 67(11):934 – 946, 2009. Special issue on Sonic Interaction Design.

137. L. Turchet, M. Marchal, A. Lécuyer, R. Nordahl, and S. Serafin. Influence of auditory and visual feedback for perceiving walking over bumps and holes in desktop VR. In *Proc. ACM Symposium on Virtual Reality Software and Technology*, pages 139–142, New York, NY, 2010. ACM.

138. L. Turchet, R. Nordahl, S. Serafin, A. Berrezag, S. Dimitrov, and V. Hayward. Audio-haptic physically-based simulation of walking on different grounds. In *Proc. IEEE Int. Workshop on Multimedia Signal Processing*, pages 269–273, 2010.

139. L. Turchet, S. Serafin, S. Dimitrov, and R. Nordahl. Conflicting audio-haptic feedback in physically based simulation of walking sounds. In *Proc. Int. Conf. on Haptic and Audio Interaction Design*, pages 97–106, Berlin, Heidelberg, 2010. Springer-Verlag.

140. G. Tzanetakis, R. Jones, C. Castillo, L. Martins, L. Teixeira, and M. Lagrange. Interoperability and the Marsyas 0.2 runtime. In *Proc. of Int. Computer Music Conf.*, Belfast, UK, 2008.

141. V. Välimäki, F. Fontana, J. O. Smith, and U. Zölzer. Introduction to the special issue on virtual analog audio effects and musical instruments. *IEEE Transactions on Audio, Speech and Language Processing*, 18:713–714, May 2010.

142. Y. Visell, F. Fontana, B. Giordano, R. Nordahl, S. Serafin, and R. Bresin. Sound design and perception in walking interactions. *International Journal of Human-Computer Studies*, 67(11):947 – 959, 2009. Special issue on Sonic Interaction Design.

143. R. Vitale and R. Bresin. Emotional cues in knocking sounds. In *Proc. Int. Conf. on Music Perception and Cognition*, Sapporo, Japan, 2008.

144. G. Wakefield, J. Kuchera-Morin, M. Novak, D. Overholt, L. Putnam, J. Thompson, and W. Smith. The AlloBrain: an interactive stereographic, 3D audio immersive environment. In *Proc. CHI Workshop on Sonic Interaction Design*, pages 59–64, Florence, Italy, 2008.

145. D. Wang and G. Brown. *Computational auditory scene analysis: principles, algorithms and applications*. IEEE Press / Wiley-Interscience, 2006.

146. H. Westerkamp. Soundwalking. *Sound Heritage*, 3(4), 1974.

147. H. Yao and V. Hayward. An experiment on length perception with a virtual rolling stone. In *Proc. of Eurohaptics*, pages 325–330, 2006.

148. S. Zambon, H. Lehtonen, and B. Bank. Simulation of piano sustain-pedal effect by parallel second-order filters. In *Proc. Conf. on Digital Audio Effects*, pages 199–204, Helsinki, Finland, 2008.